CHUI

By

Jack Cunningham

Copyright 2014

Acknowledgements

At the top of the list is my significant other, Jerrine Witt. She has been a continuing encouragement to me and a good sounding board for ideas regarding this story. She edited and corrected my manuscripts and was a constant, patient partner while I spent hours at the computer.

All my family were supportive, especially daughters, Cheryl and Pam and my sister, Susie and step daughter, Cindy Arnold and step son Terry Witt. Cousin Sara Burns did yeoman's work doing the editing and offering suggestions to enhance my story.

Father Frank was a real person. I plucked him from a lounge in Santa Fe and redressed him for this story

Finally, all my old buddies in the old 510th AF Band at Laughlin AF Base in Del Rio, Texas, and many other musicians I have played with here and there over the years. Although I have changed their names, they gave me some good characters because they were characters.

Prologue

And it came to pass on this Christmas morning a boy child was born. And, he was called Jesus. But, though he was given this name, taken from his father's Spanish heritage, his family believed it to be prudent to offer up a pseudonym, otherwise known in this modern time as a "nick name". And so it came to be that he typically would not be called Jesus, which is pronounced in Spanish as HEY SUS, but henceforth would be known as CHUI. It would be spoken as though describing something difficult to chew. In English, it would sound like CHEWY. And so, from this day forward, the baby would forever be known as Chui.

The date is December 25, 1950.

Chapter 1

The melody is stuck in his head and just won't go away. The harder he tries, the more it sticks. *"Start spreadin' the news. I'm leavin' today. I want to be a part of it -- New York – New York."*

"I hate that friggin' song! And I didn't even like the friggin' city much either" He thought to himself. But his brain just wouldn't let go of it. *"I want to wake up in that city that never sleeps."* The tune droned on in his head – driving him crazy -- no letup.

He seems to be in no hurry. He is ambling along, but his gate is unsteady as he wanders from one side to the other of the narrow, dirty alley. It is dusk, so the light is dim with single, bare light bulbs periodically lighting the rear doors of some of the buildings, reflecting the trash dumpsters, garbage cans and little puddles of water here and there. His curly, graying hair hasn't seen shampoo, a comb or a haircut for weeks. He wears no hat and his hair sticks out in all directions. His face hasn't touched a razor for days. He looks older than he is. He is probably six feet tall but has rounded shoulders. He has worn a tenor saxophone around his neck for a lot of years and thousands of songs. It has taken its toll on his posture. That saxophone is in its case and he carries it in his right hand as he stumbles along, occasionally swearing to himself as he accidentally bumps one of the smelly dumpsters with his shoulder.

He wears stained, wrinkled, khaki trousers and old tennis shoes that need new laces. His heavy blue overcoat has big pockets. His left hand fishes out a nearly empty vodka bottle, still in its paper bag. He stops, leans against a dumpster and drains the last few drops into his mouth then tosses it over his shoulder toward the trash container. He misses. The glass bottle smashes and shatters as it hits the hard surface of the alley. "So I'm not Michael Jordan". He grins with a silly smirk and shrugs his shoulders and looks around as though someone might have seen him. He giggles a superficial laugh. He doesn't care.

He has been playing his saxophone on a street corner where passers-by throw a few coins into his sax case. *"I played pretty damn lousy today,"* He thinks to himself. But he doesn't care about that either. *"I play pretty damn lousy every day. That's nothing new! I really don't give a crap! I just don't care any more. I sure wish I could get that damn song out of my mind."* It was the last song he had played today. But it had, at least, gotten him a few more tips. People loved that song even if he didn't.

Eventually he reaches *Bob's Booze Barn*. "Gimmey a pint," he slurs his words as he retrieves some coins from his pocket and dumps them on the counter. Some of the coins fall on the floor and Bob picks them up for him.

"Not enough for a pint today, buddy. How 'bout a half-pint?" Bob knows him. He is a regular. "That'll leave you enough for a little something to eat, my friend. I think you better eat something, don't you?"

"Ash okay. Thanks, Man. I 'preciate it." He tries to act straight but he hiccups and suppresses a big burp. He doesn't fool anyone.

Bob rakes the right change from his pile and hands him a half-pint of vodka in a brown paper bag. He puts his remaining change back in his pocket and heads for McDonalds on the next corner.

"Ya can't come in here, Muchacho. I told ya. Ya scare away da customers. Gimmy your money and go around to da drive up window and I'll have your Big Mac ready for ya."

"Ash good. Thanks." He spreads out some coins. Hiccups again and bumps his sax case on a chair as he pushes out the door and staggers around to the drive up window. "I didn't mean t' scare people. I just wanted t' talk t' someone." He mumbles to himself as he turns and walks outside and around the corner. He feels the embarrassment as he tries to remember the incident. His Big Mac is ready and he opens it up and takes a big bite and drops some tomato and crumbs on the ground. A car full of kids pulls in behind him and honks at him. He is startled and jumps at the unexpected sound. They laugh at him. He moves out of their way and goes behind the building and sets his sax down for a moment. He retrieves his bottle and screws off the cap. "Ahhh," he sighs, as he downs two big gulps and puts it back in his pocket.

There is a brisk wind this evening. It's always windy in West Texas in March. His old blue overcoat feels good. It is an Air Force issue with the imprint of long since removed master sergeant's stripes on each sleeve. He is weaving down the sidewalk, eating as he walks. He swallows the last of his Big Mac and pulls the bottle from his coat again, leans against a tree and stops to have another drink, then caps it and puts it back in the paper bag in his pocket. He wants to believe one more drink will help him focus his eyes and keep his balance – He knows it won't and it doesn't. He is drunk -- again.

Somehow he manages to stagger to his destination -- a doorway – an entrance to an abandoned old building. It's stark and dark and dirty in there – but he is happy to get into his little cave without getting in trouble or falling down.

He settles back out of the wind and uncorks his bottle again. One more drink. "Ahhh..." He puts the nearly empty glass vodka bottle on the steps, props himself up against his sax case and lets his vodka-laden mind wander. What might happen if he died? Would anyone come and claim him? No one knows where he is. He doesn't want anybody to know. He thinks that probably it doesn't matter much; no one cares. He often had thoughts of suicide. He was so ashamed of his miserable life -- ruined by that shit he just gulped down -- but he couldn't stop drinking. He tried. Maybe he could just cut back – little at a time – but it was always just one more. Just one more, then things would be fine again. *"Maybe this is a really good night to end this misery."* He didn't want to die but he didn't want to live either.

"King of the hill – Top of the heap. Damn I hate that friggin'song!"

He passed out and fell asleep.

****

The morning sun almost blinded his bloodshot eyes as he slowly opened them. *"Damn. That sun is sure bright this morning. Jesus, I feel like hell,"* he thinks. He spies the vodka bottle laying beside him on the step. *"There's a little bit left in there. Might as well finish it off."* He makes short work of the remnants of the clear liquid booze that he so needs in his lonely, homeless life.

His eyes cleared a little and the alcohol seemed to give him a bit of energy as he struggled to stand up. He is remembering those thoughts from the previous night. Maybe this would be a good day to give that some honest consideration. He sat down on the step and held the empty glass vodka bottle up and let the morning sunlight shine through it. *"I could break this bottle and use the*

8

sharp edge right there on my wrist. It wouldn't hurt long. Por que no? It's a good a time as any!" He lowered the bottle and was about to draw it back and smash it against the concrete step. He stopped in mid air. *"Maybe I should leave a note. What the hell am I gonna write on? What the hell am I gonna write with? What the hell am I going to say?"* There would be one last excuse for reconsideration before executing what was likely to be the final act of his life.

Then he saw it. He was peering through the glass bottle. It seemed to magnify something in the distance. It looked like a big manila envelope lying there just inside his little doorway. He sat the empty bottle down and duck-waddled toward the envelope, retrieved it, peeped out from his doorway and glanced up and down the street. No one was there. He started talking to himself. "I'll just have a look at that envelope. Maybe it belongs t' someone. Somebody probably dropped it. Let's see what's in it." There was nothing written on it. It wasn't sealed. The clasp was hooked. It would be easy to open and then close again. It was full of something! He looked around once again to see if anyone was watching. No one was. He slowly squeezed the clasp open and pulled back the flap.

"My God," he said out loud. "It's fulla money!" He looked up and down the street once more to see if anyone saw him or heard him, stuffed it under his overcoat and quickly crawled on his knees back into his doorway where no one could see him. He pulled out some of the bills.

"Hundreds, they're all hundreds. Just look at 'em. They're real, too. He mumbled to himself as he held a couple of the bills up to the sun to check the watermarks. Licking his thumb and finger, he began to count the hundred dollar bills out into little piles of twenty-five each, sticking the edges under his sax case so they couldn't blow away. His heart was pounding now from excitement. He began to mumble to himself. "Let's see, I got twenty piles and each one has twenty-five bills. That's twenty five hundred 'n each pile." He did some quick math in his head.

"Holy Jesus, Mary and Joseph!"   His words echoed through his little doorway. He jumped up and took another quick look out onto the street. He looked down at his little piles of money once again. He couldn't believe his fortune, but there it was, right there in front of him on his little step in his little doorway. "I can't believe this. I was about ready to check out of this world and now looky here. I've got fifty thousand damn dollars!"

Chapter 2

The grungy-looking, homeless man in the doorway gathered the little piles of money from beneath his saxophone case. He shuffled the green, one hundred dollar bills back to their original stack and stuffed them back in the yellow envelope, all $50,000. He opened his saxophone case and slid the envelope on top of the gold-plated instrument, shut the case and snapped the fasteners. He double-checked to see that they were securely latched. This would be no time for the case to come open accidentally.

"I've gotta think about this for a little while. I wish I hadn't finished that vodka off quite so quickly. Right now I need another drink." He kicked the empty bottle into the corner of his doorway, as if to clear away the suicidal thoughts forever.

The Texas sky was bright and sunny this late March morning and the wind had died down and it was cool, but pleasant. "This is gonna be a really good day. I sure don't want to die right now." He spoke the words out loud and then looked around to see if anyone had heard him. They had not. "It certainly has started off pretty well," he said, and then chuckled to himself. *"I guess I'd better see if I can figure out whose money this is and where it came from."*

But, then, he rationalized. Maybe it was drug money that was dropped for a pickup. He certainly didn't want to get involved in that. Or maybe it fell out of an airplane, he mused. Or maybe he was just trying to figure a way to justify keeping it. Maybe? Probably! *"Hell, it's my money; I found it, didn't I? Life was so simple before this morning. I guess that's what they mean when they say money's the root of all evil. My life is already gettin' complicated and I've only been rich for an hour."* He laughed at himself again. *"Guess I better have some breakfast."* Then he suddenly realized, *"Well, crap, if I give someone a hundred dollar bill for breakfast they will swear I stole it and call the cops. Now what do I do? I've got fifty thousand damn dollars and can't afford to buy my friggin' breakfast!"*

He opened his case again and fished around in the corners where the folks had thrown their change. Maybe there were some coins that he hadn't used for the vodka and Big Mac. He found some. *"Guess I'd better use this for my breakfast."* He dumped the coins in his pocket, counting them as he put them in. He counted six dollars and thirty cents in coins.

"I'd better get out of this doorway before someone comes along and gets me for loitering or vagrancy. This is no day for that!" He was mumbling to himself again. He got up from his doorway, snatched his sax case by the handle and ambled down the street in the warm, Texas sunshine, leaving his filthy, depressing home for the last time. He looked up at the blue Texas sky and smiled to himself. For once in a long time, he was walking without staggering.

His favorite liquor store was only a few blocks away. He thought he had better use some of his change to get his morning bottle of vodka. Then, uncharacteristically, he stopped in his tracks. *"Hold on! I can't do that! I can't have any booze right now. I gotta* wait." He wanted a drink in the worst way but he struggled with himself. *"I'll just wait a bit -- just a little while. I need to keep my mind straight. I won't get the vodka just yet. I'll just – uh – I'll just get some breakfast first. Yeah – that's what I'll do. I'll just get some breakfast first. Maybe that will clear up my brain a little. That'll make me think better about what to do with all this money! – All this money! – I've never had this much money in my life!"* He was thinking to himself as he strolled down the street with his sax case in his right hand. "But, it's not mine, not really, it must belong to somebody. No one would just drop it there. Someone must have lost it. I guess I better try to figure out who it belongs to." The weight of the problem was beginning to get to him. He was muttering away to himself. And so he walked on down the street right past the liquor store and made a left turn and headed toward McDonalds.

"They probably won't let me come in," he thought. *"But I am going inside today. I am just going to walk right in the front door and see what happens."* He had suddenly gained a measure of confidence he hadn't had for a long time.

And so as he approached the big arches, he was determined to carry out his promise and walk right in the front door. With his overcoat on and his sax case in hand, with $50,000 in it, he did it. He threw back his shoulders and walked right in. His head was high today and he thought to himself, *"I could buy lots and lots of Big Macs today, if I really wanted to. If they don't want my business, I'll go someplace else."*

And, with that attitude, he got in line and ordered a Big Mac and a cup of black coffee and dropped the exact change on the counter. The manager, who had refused to serve him before, glanced at him out of the corner of his eye.

"Here it comes." They are going to make me leave."

But, it was not so. He paid with his change; they handed him his food and said nothing. He took his tray and found a table, put his saxophone on the adjoining chair and sat down. *"I guess I can eat inside today; they must have had a change of heart, or, maybe I just look a little more confident. I feel a little different. It feels good. It must be the money; makes a guy feel like he is worth something."* Then he began to debate with himself, again. *"But, it's not mine. It's not my money. Well, I guess it's my money for now,"* he argued. *"What the hell am I supposed to do? I am really confused."*

He ate his Big Mac and drank his coffee. He looked around and smiled at some of the customers and they smiled back. *"This is nice, this is really nice,"* he said to himself. He noticed that no one sat close to him. Then he glanced around the room. When no one was looking, he sniffed at himself. *"Whew! No wonder no one wants to sit close to me, I really stink."*

"Know what I think I am going to do?" He asked himself the question, as though he didn't know the answer. *"I am going to take a shower and clean up a little!"* He answered his own question. He would need to find a nice hotel. *"Nothing fancy -- nothing fancy,"* he thought, *"just a regular little cheap hotel. I'll just get out one of the hundred dollar bills -- just one."* The debate continued. *"I certainly have that coming, don't I? I mean I know they'll give me a reward when I return the money. So they wouldn't begrudge me just one hundred dollar bill. After all, there are 500 -- hundred dollar bills in there. I just need a shower and shave and maybe a place to sleep tonight, maybe in a real bed. Maybe even a TV. Wouldn't that be just great? That would be just OK. That would be just OK."* He smiled and nodded a few times in response.

He got so excited he almost talked out loud. *"I'd better not talk to myself. They might think I am drunk again and kick me out. I better just keep quiet and just eat my Big Mac."*

"Chi-wa-wa!" An old Mexican expression came blasting through his brain. *"I am so happy, I*

think I better go back *to that liquor store and get me a ------!"* Then he stopped in mid sentence. He chastised himself very quickly. *"NO, NO, I can't do that. Not yet, anyway."* He started to argue with himself again. *"Wouldn't it be really nice to drink my booze and fall asleep in a real bed? No, No, I better not do that either. It sounds like such a good idea. I could get it and save it for later. That would be nice. That's a good idea – but I don't think so. If I get a bottle, I'll drink it, won't I? I might do something stupid with all this money. I better skip that. Let's just put that idea on hold for now."*

So many thoughts were swirling around in his vodka-laden mind as he finished his Big Mac and drank his coffee. He had had such a lonely life for many months, but at least there was no responsibility. Now he was suddenly overcome with decisions.

"Let me see, let me see. The money is inside of an envelope, which is inside my sax case. I can't just open it up right here. That certainly would attract attention. Maybe I could put it on my lap and open it up – No, that won't work either, it's too big. Maybe I could go into the rest room. No, sure as hell someone would come in." His anxiety level was off the chart.

He finished his burger and coffee, stuffed the paper wrapper and empty cup in the bag, got up and headed towards the trashcan. *"Jesus!"* He stopped in his tracks. *"I can't leave my sax case lying on that chair, not even for a second. It's got*

$50,000 in it." He suddenly became very paranoid. He stepped back and grabbed his case and put the wadded up bag in the trash, and ran out the door and onto the sidewalk.

He was confused and wasn't sure where he was going. He ambled down the street, and without realizing it, headed toward his corner. It was the place he had played his sax and panhandled for change for the past several months. It was his place of business, his "office." City officials looked the other way and let him panhandle there. They considered it as "entertainment," rather than panhandling. There was a nice familiar feel and smell to it. It was as though he owned that corner and he was drawn toward it without thinking where he was going.

When he came to his senses, he was there. His mind was clearing a little. *"I know,"* he thought, *"I can just open up my sax case as usual and quickly take out the envelope with the money and roll it up and put it in my big overcoat pocket and pretend like everything is normal. No one will know what it is. Then I can play just like I always have. I had better do what I always do, so no one will be suspicious. Then I can wait til dark and slip some money out and find a hotel."*

He was content with his decision. He was excited about his plan for the day. He got out his old golden Selmer saxophone. Subliminally, he licked the reed and placed it in the ligature then wiggled the mouthpiece on the instrument just like

17

he had done thousands of times. He chuckled to himself as he hung the sax on the strap around his neck, jiggled his fingers over the keys and prepared to play his first tune. He didn't care if anyone gave him a dime today. He thought how many times he came away with little or no change and today he just didn't give a damn. He was going to play for the shear pleasure and enjoyment of the music. He was going to play for his own pleasure. And so he did.

"I think I will play some nice old slow, melancholy songs today," he thought, *"I think I will play 'Sophisticated Lady.'"* He raised his sax to his mouth, took a big breath, closed his eyes and began to play the old Duke Ellington tune. The notes came out so nice and clear. He played it through one time and decided to play a second chorus. This time he began to improvise, holding a note into the next measure or shortening a phrase here and there. His eyes remained tightly closed as he played. His mind wandered as he thought about the hundreds of times he had played that tune and the good times and the bad times. He thought about the booze and the smoke and the bars. He thought about how many recording studios he had been in – how many recordings he must have been a part of that no one ever knew about. It amazed him how he could let his mind stray so far away and never miss a note of the song. He had put himself in a trance for a few minutes as he played his tune. His mind suddenly "woke up." And, for a split second, had to think what song he was playing and where he was. He

realized he had nearly finished and was ready for the closing bars.

He didn't care if anyone else liked his rendition; he just played from his soul. He finished with a nice flourish with an arpeggio, holding out the last note like it was to be his last. He opened his eyes and couldn't believe what he saw. A crowd of maybe 10 or 12 people had gathered and was clapping their hands, cheering and dropping money into his sax case.

"Play Alley Cat," a girl's voice shouted.

His thoughts went to an old musician buddy who once told him, "You can't make any money if you can't play 'Alley Cat." He hated the song, but decided to take his friend's advice and go with the moment. *"At least she didn't ask for New York New York," he* thought to himself. Putting the sax mouthpiece back between his lips, he wailed out his best schmaltzy rendition of Alley Cat, as he bounced his head up and down, did a little dance and listened to the crowd cheer him on. He heard money being dropped into his "kitty."

Then a man's deep, resonant voice from somewhere said, "Hey, man, how about 'Body and Soul'?"

He couldn't believe his ears. No one ever wanted to hear "Body and Soul." It was a very complicated song that only the best sax players would even try to play. He would normally not even try. But today was different. He thought, "What the hell." He looked around to see who had asked for the song. He saw a white-haired, bearded, priest, dressed in his classic black suit with the traditional white collar. He pointed his finger at him, as if to ask if it was he who made the request. The priest nodded his head in the affirmative. He thought that was an odd request for a priest, but he leaned his head toward the old priest and whispered, "I'll give it a try."

"Bless you, my son. You'll do well."

He had not played that song for years. *"It's like riding a bike,"* he remembered the old adage, *"You never forget how."* Hoping that adage was true, he closed his eyes tightly again and began to wail out the first few measures of the song. *"I guess it doesn't matter if I play it well or not,"* he was thinking as he played. *"I don't care whether they give me any tips today or not. They'll probably all go away, anyway."* He played on, his eyes closed tightly, wrinkling his brow and keeping time with his left foot, as he played. *"Wow, this tune is going pretty well. I sound damn good if I do say so myself."* He was playing and thinking at the same time. His agile fingers were pressing down on all the right keys. He slipped into the "bridge" with its complicated key change to sharps and then to flats, not missing a single note. He remembered the song well and played a second chorus and improvised, getting further and further away from the melody but never departing from the chord structure. The song rang out. He grew more

20

confident. He was blowing up a storm. The last few bars of the tune ended with a beautiful obbligato and finally the last note faded into the sunny Texas morning. He opened his eyes and heard nothing -- just silence. The crowd was still there, even more people had gathered. They were almost in a trance. But, they were as quiet as mice. Finally the young woman, who had requested Alley Cat, broke the silence. "My God -- that was beautiful!" she whispered. She was nearly moved to tears. She could not have given him enough money to top those five words. He was paid for his song in full many times over. The old priest was nowhere to be seen.

Chapter 3 -- Laughlin Air Force Base, Texas – 1948

To say that Del Rio, Texas was *just* a dusty little town on the Mexican border along the Rio Grande River, was an understatement in 1948. Although that was *true* in 1948, virtually the entire USA had, literally *heard* of Del Rio. Not because it was a little dusty town, but because of the gigantic radio station a mile or so across the Rio Grande River in Old Mexico. Villa Acuna was the small Mexican border town where the owners of XERF Radio had placed the transmitter so as to sidestep the rules and regulations of the United States Federal Communications Commission. Not only was that radio station able to emit a signal hundreds of times stronger than allowed in the U S, but Dr. Brinkley's Kansas descendants were able to continue to hawk the "goat gland" extract for erectile dysfunction. Then there was the "prayer cloth" to place on your radio to get your problems healed by placing your hands on the radio. And don't forget the plastic Jesus icon for your dashboard to protect you from harm while driving. That spawned a short-lived hit song, an irreverent spoof: *"I don't care if it rains or freezes -- long as I got my plastic Jesus –there on the dashboard of my car!"*

Paul Callenger would pitch the questionable, mostly religious merchandise each night as the powerful radio signal sped around the world seven times every second. He would coerce listeners into sending their hard-earned cash to "X-ER-F –

DEEELL REEEO – TEXAS. He could spit out the address into his powerful microphone as no other human could. Poor, superstitious, religious folks would be taken in by the too-good-to-be-true solutions for their ills, wants and needs. The dollars would roll in by the thousands to a guarded room at the Roosevelt Hotel in downtown Del Rio.

Del Rio, Texas, was known throughout the land, thanks to that radio station just across the Mexican border.

But most people had no idea, nor did they care, where it was or what it was or who lived in this West Texas town about 100 miles from San Antonio situated on the Rio Grande River. Its local claim to fame is a fresh water spring situated in a park in the center of town. "San Felipe Spring," it is called. History tells us, according to the sign near the spring, that it was a watering hole for the camel corps that was stationed in West Texas in the early development of the United States. Yes, there were camels in the US western desert back in the 1800's. They were stationed at Fort Clark, about 20 miles southeast of Del Rio. Today, Brackettville is the leftover village from that era. The famous John Wayne movie, "The Alamo," was filmed there. A well-worn sign still invites tourists to visit the exact movie-set replica of the Alamo that still remains.

In 1948, the war was long over. The BIG war folks called it – World War II. The US government had seen fit to give the Air Corps its own designation. What formerly was the Army Air Corps with its brown and khaki uniforms and brown caps and brown shoes, had become the US Air Force. The uniform was now blue, like the blue sky. Or, like the new fight song says -- "Wild Blue Yonder." They were to be called "Airmen" instead of "Soldiers." And they would sing, *Off we go into the wild blue yonder, flying high into the sun..."*

Laughlin Air Force Base was created to teach new pilots how to fly big B-26 bombers. Even though the war was over, the U S Government was not going to allow another Pearl Harbor to happen – ever again. The hundreds of men, who were the accountants, cooks, mechanics, and scores of other behind-the-scenes personnel, were about to be sent to this outpost to see to it that these Air Force future pilots had the best support possible.

It was to be a part of the Training Command Wing of the Air Force. These sparsely populated, tumbleweed-covered surroundings were perfect for learning to fly, and to drop practice bombs onto this desolate part of the United States.

There were few residents in those years. Most of them were of Mexican descent. The area was a part of Mexico at one time in its history. A narrow bridge crosses the river and separates the two countries. Both Mexican and US Customs guard it. They seldom check anyone. They recognize most people by sight. A few workers or tourists cross the bridge each day. It is anything but a tourist Mecca. Most of the residents of this place work in some vocation allied to agriculture. That was about to change.

This desolate area next to the Rio Grande River on the Mexican border, which was selected to train pilots, was in the West Texas wide-open spaces, just outside Del Rio, Texas.

Chapter 4 -- Eglin Air Force Base, Florida. -- 1948

At the same time in history, about 2000 miles east of Laughlin Air Force Base, Texas, the beautiful Florida sun is shining at Eglin Air Force Base near Ft. Walton Beach. Cali Williams is sitting on the Florida beach with her mother. She is nearly sixteen. Her name is Caliente, meaning "warm" in Spanish. Her dad had liked the name when he heard her Cuban-born hospital nurse called that by an Army doctor. He borrowed the name from her.

Dad had joined the Army Air Corps as soon as he was graduated from Butler University in Indiana. He had majored in music and planned to teach music, but the Selective Service was about to get him so he joined the Air Corps to beat the "draft" and the dreaded Army infantry. Jim Williams is a Tech Sergeant in the new Air Force.

The surf from the Gulf of Mexico smacks onto the shore as young Cali romps in the waves, screaming when they hit her a little harder than she expects. Susie Williams is watching her daughter, trying to find just the right words to tell her daughter something she did not want to hear. Cali was so happy in Florida. She was doing quite well in school, making nearly straight A's. The small high school was attended by mostly air base kids. There were only a handful of "minorities." Blacks and Hispanics were mostly confined to their own areas of town and that did not include the

26

base. Cali was such a beautiful girl with long blond hair, blowing in the Gulf breeze. She had developed a slim and sensuous figure in the last few months. She was very much aware of it but pretended that she had not noticed how she attracted glances from men of all sizes and shapes as they passed by. She looked older than her fifteen years.

Now, Susie Williams is going to need to accomplish her mission for the day. She has brought Cali to the beach ostensibly to give her a nice afternoon doing what she loved to do, play in the Gulf. But that is only an excuse. She is trying to figure out a way to tell her only daughter that she is going to be moving away from her friends and her wonderful school. She is going to have to tell her in a very few minutes that she is going to be moving from this beautiful white sandy beach in Florida. She is going to turn Cali's world upside down very shortly. She must tell her she will be moving way out west, hundreds of miles from the nearest body of water. She must somehow find an easy way to say to her; "We are going to be in Florida for only a few more months. We are moving out west. Daddy has been reassigned to Laughlin Air Force Base in a place called Del Rio, Texas."

Chapter 5 -- 1948

"Iturria Ranch" --The big, weatherworn sign hangs proudly on the big wide, iron gate leading down a road to somewhere too far to see. The sign announces the entrance to the "Iturria Ranch" but the owner is no longer called Iturria, although the family has not changed. The ranch owner is now Paco Vasquez. The Vasquez name has been used since one of the Iturrias a few generations ago had no sons. There was only a daughter who was called Dona Maria Iturria. She married a ranch hand called Pablo Dominguez Vasquez. And so the "begats" began with the Vasquez name for many decades. And that brings us up to 1948.

The ranch property was said to be nearly 400 years old, from an old Spanish Land Grant given to the Iturria family for their loyalty in spreading Christianity to the "heathen savages" who dared to practice their own thousand-year-old beliefs. But today, in 1948, it belongs to the Vasquez family. Paco is the patriarch, the "Jefe." His wife is Aranda Cantu, daughter of Enrique, a local feed-store owner. Her brother is Father Raul Cantu, the local Padre at "Lady of Guadalupe." Paco and Aranda were married by her brother over 23 years ago at the local mission.

Their youngest son is 16 now. His name is Juan Jesus. However, his middle name is seldom used. Being the youngest, everyone calls him Juanito. His "Anglo" friends call him Johnny. There are two older twin brothers and one sister.

"Life is good today." The man looked up at the clear blue Texas sky above the mountains as he walked. "Life is wonderful today. There is nothing like a good gig to make you feel good. You can get a genuine high on music. I haven't had that for so long." He let his mind wander back as he walked. "I can't remember the last time I played so well." He was talking out loud to himself. He had played his tenor saxophone on his corner for several hours today. He had not played so well for a long time. It is hard to play well when the player is drunk. Today was different. The player was sober. People came and went today, but they all were appreciative and generous. They didn't just pass by. They stopped for a while, talked, and listened to his mellow music. They applauded, making him play even better. He had counted the tips after he decided to stop playing for the day and move on. He had over $60 in change and bills. He didn't often get bills. He could get his motel and maybe he wouldn't need to get into his envelope after all. He stuck his hand in his pocket and checked the envelope again.

Up ahead he could see a couple of motel signs in the distance. There it was, coming into view, Motel 6. It didn't look too expensive as he drew closer. He walked up and peered in the glass front door and saw the clerk behind the counter. He appeared to be a foreigner of some sort. He had on a white turban. Entering the door, he sat his sax case on the floor and put his foot on it. "How much for a room?"

"Fo-ty-five dollahs, including tax for a single vit one bed." The man answered him with a clipped dialect that sounded like he was from somewhere else.

"You a Muslim?"

"I am *not!*" The man snapped back, apparently irritated by the question. "I am a Hindu from Injia, and I own this motel. Does that mattah to you?"

"No. Sorry. It's the turban. Just curious. I didn't mean anything; it just slipped out. That's OK."

"What's OK? -- That I am a Hindu -- or that I own the motel -- or that you want the room?" The man laughed. Then, so did the clerk. He realized he had sounded rather sharp. He didn't mean to.

"All of the above."

"OK, will that be cash or charge?"

The man fished $45 of his tip money out of his pocket and laid it on the counter.

"I need a razor; do you have one I could borrow?"

"Let's just say I like the way you play 'Body and Soul'. I was especially impressed with the way you handled that bridge. You know -- the sharps and flats. That's a pretty tough tune. Now, do you want the gig or not?"

"I don't know. How do you know me?"

"Cause, man, I heard you play today."

"Wait a minute. You aren't a priest, are you?"

"Could be. Now, do you want the gig, man?"

"Well, -- uh sure. Sure. But I don't have any clothes or -- "

"I'll take care of that. You have enough bread to hold you over at that motel?"

"How did you know where I was?"

"Never mind that. Let's see, this is Friday. I'll need you tomorrow night. I will call the hotel and pay for a few nights and leave some money with the manager for you to go get some threads tomorrow. Then I'll pick you up about 6. That'll give us time to get across the border by 8. This place is right across the bridge. It doesn't take long to get there once we get across. Oh, one more thing. Stay off the vodka! No more sauce!"

"How did you know --?"

"I know a lot of things. See ya tomorrow at 6!" He hung up.

"Holy shit! What a day! I woke up this morning, a homeless drunk, about ready to cash it in, and now I've got $50,000 in cash, I'm sleeping in a real bed watching TV and I've got a real job. Almost makes me believe in all that crap the priests and nuns taught me -- it *did* start with a friggin' priest. I feel like a little kid. I feel like jumping up and down on this bed. Damn, I wish I had a drink."

Chapter 9 – Autumn -- 1948

"Que es? What the hell is that?" Paco was running from under his big ranch house porch and looking up at the sky above his pasture. "It looks like a big Murceilago de plato, a beeg silver bat!" It was an autumn Sunday afternoon in 1948 and the Vasquez family had returned from Mass and were all sitting around relaxing after dinner and reading the Sunday Edition of the San Antonio *Light*.

"I was just reading about the new trainers they are getting here at the Air Base," Juanito was showing his father. "Look, Papa, there is a picture in the paper. Those are T-33's. They are the new jet trainer planes. It says they are starting to come in this weekend for the pilots to train in. Pilots are going to learn to fly jet planes here in Del Rio." Juanito was excited at the prospect of something new to see. He was nearly 17 now and a handsome young man with jet black, curly hair. He was near the top of his junior class at Del Rio High. He was to be in the graduating class of 1950. He could hardly believe that he would be graduating in just one more year. It seemed like his school years flew by. He had thought about what he wanted to do when he graduated -- a lawyer, maybe -- not a doctor. He didn't like blood much. His grade point was 3.8, good enough to get into most any Texas university. His family could afford to send him about anywhere he wanted to go. He thought

about A & M over in College Station. That was a
long way off. Maybe he could go to a junior
college and then transfer. He hadn't been away
from home much in his life. He had a few months
to decide. But those new jet trainers sure did look
like something he might like to learn more about.
He went outside and shaded his eyes as four more
came over and peeled off into the landing pattern.
"Man, that looks like fun," he thought to himself.
"That sure looks like fun."

But, right now he was thinking he ought to
be interested in having some fun and going out
with a few girls. He thought about that new blond
girl that sat across from him in History class, but
she was a little snobby and he was very shy. She
had just moved to Del Rio. She made it a point to
let everyone know she was from Florida. Her dad
was stationed at Laughlin, he had heard. She sure
acted sexy – really liked those tight skirts and
sweaters. She kind of swished her behind when
she walked. He thought she might have been
watching him out of the corner of her eye. Juanito
thought he needed to meet her and maybe ask her
out. They call her Cali. He wondered where she
got such a name. Only problem – he was terribly
shy -- this was Del Rio, Texas in 1948 – she was a
blond, light skinned Anglo and he was not.

Chapter 10

The move from Ft. Walton Beach in Florida had been a tough one. Jim Williams had needed to go on ahead to Del Rio and take up residence at Laughlin Air Base alone for a while. They had made him a Master Sergeant and put him in charge of all the "facilities" at the base. He was in charge of the Airman's club, the movie theater, the beer garden, the golf course and the small recreational area at Lake Walk. Military personnel who are stationed in these areas far away from "civilization" are given a few extra benefits. Laughlin was considered an "outpost." So the U S Air Force had seen fit to put someone in charge of all the entertainment for the troops. Jim had a degree in music and so when he joined the Army Air Corps back in 1944, he was assigned to provide entertainment for the guys at their training bases. That was the assignment he had ever since.

But, he was also a good trumpet and piano player. So, he frequently was able to play with a combo at the Officer's or the NCO club for a little extra money. He especially loved to play New Orleans "Dixieland" music and had a group in Florida called the "Dixiecats." Now that he was stationed in Del Rio at Laughlin, he poked around and tried to find some musicians to start another little combo.

He found a trombone player whose name was Chuck Berghetti. Chuck was a skinny little guy who worked in the payroll department. He was from Philadelphia.

The clarinet player was a Latino. He was Alfredo Baca. Everyone called him Freddie. He learned to play Dixieland while he was stationed in New Orleans while he was in the Army. He could be called "Freddie" when he was playing with the guys, but when he was on duty at the base, he was Captain Baca. He was a flight instructor.

The bass player, Ward Perkins, was a country musician who led a double life. He was a local, and played country music at a honky-tonk bar out by the river during the week, but played with Jim and the Dixiecats when he could. Ward was a superb bass player and hated country music but said it made him more money than anything else he did. He also had lots of sordid stories of young girl "groupies," which were not necessarily proven to be true but they made good tales.

When Ward could not play, a young airman by the name of Bernie Schmidt was always available. But Bernie was a pretty straight-laced guy and was married to a pretty straight-laced girl who was very religious and only let him out if it was necessary and the money was good.

Although Jim was capable of playing the piano, he much preferred to play the trumpet. The piano player was a heavyset Staff Sergeant. He was Bob Seagrove. He had a Doctor of Music degree from Eastman. He had written a symphony for his dissertation. He was, somehow, sent to Laughlin Air Base in Del Rio, Texas, to be a cook. He said he enjoyed cooking and was quite good at it, but never intended to do it for a living. He had no idea how he got assigned to this job. It was a classic government screw-up. He joined the service to serve his time as a musician, but ended up in the chow hall. He was on his first hitch and was patiently waiting for the day he was finished and would be out of this zoo.

The drummer was a local guy, whose dad owned "Jack's Lounge," a local watering hole. He was Rocky Silva. His dad, Jack Silva, catered to the Air Base guys. His bar and lounge was located right on the point where Highway 90 and the road to the international bridge to Mexico came together. It was a perfect location for a restaurant and Jack did quite well. Rocky was not a particularly good drummer, but in his hip pocket he had a ready-made gig in his dad's lounge. This was the place the band played every Sunday afternoon.

With Jim Williams as the trumpet player, that was the Dixiecats at Laughlin Air Force Base in the fall of 1948.

Chapter 11

Jim had gotten the band organized and now he desperately needed to get his family organized. Susie had stayed behind to hire the movers and schedule the packing and pickup of their belongings. They lived in base housing, so there was no problem with needing to sell a house. Career service people learned not to sink too many roots and Jim had been in for two hitches and knew it was not wise to buy a house.

Since he was an NCO and now a Master Sergeant, he got a few special privileges when it came to base housing. The only problem was, at Laughlin, there was little or no regular base housing. The government had bought several "mobile homes" or "house trailers" as they were called, for base married personnel. They were all silver and various sizes but they were all perfectly lined up in rows and all exactly alike. Each had a big black number professionally painted on its front. Each one was eight feet wide and varied from 20 to 50 feet long. The longer ones had two bedrooms. They each had a bathroom with a shower and a fairly nice kitchen with a living room with a pull out couch. The dining table was retractable with a couple of extra leaves for company. They each had an awning on the front and a small lawn with a little picnic table on the patio.

This was the best Jim could do. There were a few apartments and even fewer houses in Del Rio, but the rent was exorbitant. He thought this would just have to do until he found something better. There were some very nice mobile home parks in town and the industry had begun to make some very nice "coaches," as the dealers liked to call them. Jim had looked at a few but wanted Susie and Cali to come before he made any decisions.

To say that Susie was deflated and disappointed in her new home was an understatement. But she grinned, gritted her teeth, pulled herself up by her bootstraps and made the best of it. After all, she was a career military wife.

Telling Cali that things would get better was like talking to a rock. Cali had become a cardboard cutout of her former self. She smiled, and she was polite and she was friendly and lovable to a stranger, but her mother knew the sound of that tone of voice. Cali was "sickeningly" sweet, cold and condescending. It was *"Yes, Mother. Of course, Mother, Oh, yes Daddy, I certainly will. Just tell me exactly what you want and I will do it, Mother.* Susie almost wished that Cali would get angry or sassy once in awhile, just to show she was a normal teenager.

"I am sure she will get through this," Susie Williams would try and talk to Jim at night in bed. "This trailer is so damn small you can't have a private conversation," she would say in a stage whisper. And the lovemaking wasn't so easy either. The trailer was springy and squeaky and Jim and Susie would sometimes rush home before Cali got there to have some relief from their pent up sexual frustrations.

All in all, Jim was glad, secretly, that he had some outlet once in awhile at night with his band. Susie loved for Jim to play but was getting a little aggravated at his freedom and her own imprisonment in the tiny trailer. Cali was becoming a problem waiting to happen and was getting more and more caustic and sarcastic as she played her little *"Why, Mother, whatever do you mean, I am just the sweetest thing that ever lived,"* game. Susie Williams was beginning to get to the end of her rope, and she was not able to do anything about it, and she had no one to talk to except a few neighbors whose major topic of conversation consisted of old wives' tales and how not to mark your baby when you're pregnant. Susie found 18-year-old Dovey Dale, the pregnant wife of an Airman Third Class (Buck Private) to be especially amusing. She kept thinking she should write down all the old West Virginia folklore Dovey Dale, who used two names, taught her. These tales of the mountains had, no doubt, been passed down for generations. She always thought she should write a book about Dovey Dale, but she never got around to it.

But, Susie hung in there like a good military wife, hoping for better times to come.

Chapter 12

"I should be hungry," Chui was talking to himself, "But I am so excited, I can't think about eating right now." He looked at himself in the mirror. His long nap was over. He decided it was time to get himself cleaned up. He picked up the phone and punched the 0 on the phone.

"Front desk. This is Punj."

"Hey, this is Chui in 108. I need to wash my clothes. Can you help me?"

"We don't have any laundry facilities here. Hmmm – wait a minute --I'll tell you what. My wife and I have a small apartment behind the office and we have a washer and dryer. I'll bring you a robe and you can give me your clothes and we'll wash them for you

"Man! That is really nice of you. What is your name?"

"Punj. Punjabi Gupta. Don't try to pronounce it. You can call me Punj. P-U-N-J, He spelled it. His accent spit the name right off the tip of his tongue.

Punj knocked on room 108 and Chui was ready with all his clothes in a wad. Standing stark naked, he peeped from behind the half-open door and handed his clothes out in exchange for a nice white terry cloth robe. "Thanks, man – uh -- Punj.

Thanks a lot. This is really nice of you. I can't thank you enough."

"Well, you are going to be with us for a few days, so I thought I better treat you like a good customer. An old priest dropped by and paid you up for three days and left a few bucks for you. I put the money in the pocket of your robe. By the way, you can keep the robe. I stole a bunch of them from a Hilton in Chicago. I have three or four more."

Chui did not know if he was joking or not, but he didn't care. Everything was working well right now and he didn't want to disturb anything. He checked in the pocket of the robe and found a hundred dollars in 10's and 20's. He thought about how much money that would have meant to him yesterday. But what a pittance a hundred was now. *"But it's not my money,"* he told himself once more, but was beginning not to believe it. Next step was a shower and a shave.

"Good Grief, you look younger." He admired himself in the mirror. Punj had brought the clean clothes back, as promised. They were all neatly folded. "My wife did them for you," he admitted as he stuck the pile of clothes through the opening in the door. "I wouldn't have been so neat about it."

"But this is not my shirt."

"I know, yours was pretty well beat up so I gave you one of mine. It's not exactly your style, but it doesn't have any holes in it. You can give it back when you get another one. I threw in some new underwear, too. I threw yours in the trash."

Chui was embarrassed but grateful. "Any good restaurants around here?" He changed the subject.

"Denny's is next door."

Chui's thoughts briefly considered whether he wanted to eat at a place with no booze. Then he thought about the promise he had made the priest, so he let out a big sigh and sarcastically decided it would be a *grand* idea to have his first sit down dinner in many months with no vodka, at Denny's next door. He put on his new under shorts, his old, but now clean, pants, and Punj's shirt. He sat down and put on his clean sox and old shoes. Then he looked over at his old blue overcoat and stuck his hand in the right hand pocket to touch that envelope once again. He knew it was there, but it was reassuring to feel it and its valuable cargo. It was cool enough that he could wear the coat and not look ridiculous. So he put it on and walked out the door. He headed for Denny's.

Chapter 13

"Padre Island – Padre Island? Why does that sound familiar?" Cali thought to herself when the name came up among her classmates at Del Rio High School.

"Its way down the river at Brownsville," one of her friends explained.

"Oh, yeah, I remember now. My mother was trying to convince me that moving to Del Rio was the greatest thing that would ever happen to me, she was trying to bribe me. She told me Padre Island was really close and we would go there a lot. That was a joke! So, what is it and how far away is it?" Cali asked.

"Oh, I don't know but it takes all day to get there. I've only been there once, a long time ago when I was just a kid."

"When's everyone going?"

"It's the vacation we get in the spring. I think it's sometime in March. The church is sponsoring it. But you don't have to be a Catholic. Everyone is going."

The Lady of Guadalupe Church was organizing the trip to take place in a couple of months. Many of the students were Catholics and belonged to this parish. It was, frankly, the only game in town. The old priest, Father Cantu, was getting well along in years and had managed to get a new, young priest to take over the responsibility of the youth of the church. He had come from New Orleans. Although he was younger than most new priests, he was a bright and talented young Hispanic. His name was Francisco Jimenez. He called himself Father Francisco. He had decided a trip to the Gulf might be a good, wholesome way to spend the little vacation that was coming up in the spring. Although it was sponsored and sanctioned by the Catholic Church, it was open to any high school senior who could afford the few dollars it would cost to charter the bus and buy some food.

Cali got excited about the prospect of going to a beach, even though it was not Florida and even though she had vowed not to like anything about Del Rio or the state of Texas. She had been in Del Rio over a year and had been determined not to enjoy anything. She was determined to punish her parents for dragging her away from Florida regardless of the consequences. She vowed to survive until she could get out of this horrible place.

However, she was secretly beginning to enjoy herself. But she was not about to let her parents know. One of the subjects of her attention was that rancher's young son. His dad owned that big ranch over there just north of the Air Force base. Juan Vasquez was his name. But, everyone called him Johnny. Cali thought about how good-looking he was. She wondered just how she might get him to notice her. He was in her history class and sat right across from her. She had tried to flirt with him but he seemed so shy. She was very much aware that it was not very socially acceptable to date a "Mexican" if you were an "Anglo." But that only added to the determination she had to be the rebellious teenager she was determined to be. She was trying her best to get herself into trouble if she could -- not bad trouble – just exasperating trouble. She pulled back her shoulders a little to make her breasts a little more prominent. When he was following her close by, she would swivel her backside just a little just to try to get his attention, but he was so shy, it didn't seem to be very effective. But, then, out of the blue -- *"My God, speak of the devil. There he is right there. He's coming right toward me,"* she thought to herself. She stopped in her tracks.

"Cali!" He called to her.

"Uh -- Hi, Johnny."

"Uh, Uh, Oh, Uh. What are you doing Friday?"

"Nothing, Johnny. Did you have something in mind?"

"Maybe we -- uh – I thought maybe we might go out somewhere -- maybe to a movie?"

"I would love that, Johnny. You know my dad runs the base theater. I can get us in there for free. Their movies are much better. You want to pick me up? I will have Dad leave word at the gate for the AP to let you in to get me. Does that sound OK?" Cali had accomplished her mission. She had a broad smile.

"That is super! Yeah – that is great. I'll see you tomorrow night about seven. OK? *That was easier than I thought."*

"OK Johnny -- tomorrow night at seven at my place."

Both teenagers turned in different directions and walked away from each other. But both were feeling that unexplainable rippling sensation that occurs when something new and exciting has just happened. And thus began a new chapter in the lives of two High School Seniors at Del Rio High School.

****

Winter was nearly over. Christmas had come and gone and New Years' Eve had been celebrated, bringing in the New Year and the new decade. Gone forever was the year 1949. It was 1950. Spring was coming. Although the seasonal changes were not as evident as in the north, there were some signs of spring in West Texas along the Rio Grande River.

This year, one of the signs of spring was going to be a venture down the highway that followed the Rio Grande River along the Mexican and United States borders, toward the mouth of the river and the Gulf of Mexico. That was where, millions of years ago, a 120-mile long sand bar had formed. The Spanish had called the bay between the sand bar and the shoreline Laguna Madre. And they had called the Island formed by the sand bar Padre Island; Mother Lagoon and Father Island.

Pirates, it was told, had used the island to bury treasure they had stolen from merchant ships in the Gulf. Legends abound about this long strip of sand. But in 1950 it was nearly deserted, except for its southern tip. There, Cameron County, Texas, had reserved a good-sized chunk of the sandy beach for a public park. The county had built a nice concrete covered pavilion and erected several small "cabanas," which could be rented for a very small fee. These cabanas were designed for short-time use – a day or two at most. They each had bunk beds and a sink with running cold water. There were no bathrooms – just a community bath – one for each gender. These bathrooms had a few open showers and toilets and sinks, which dispensed only sun-heated water from a big black tank atop the building. However, the public, from both Texas and Mexico, made good use of these cabanas quite regularly.

When the Lady of Guadalupe Church and the Del Rio High School senior class decided to have a spring venture to Padre Island, Cali was delirious. Not only was she going to see her precious Gulf again, she was going to be on a weekend trip with Johnny. Maybe she could break through that timid exterior and get him to warm up a little. But she dare not allow her parents to know how excited she was. It would take some acting, but she would not blow her cover and admit that she was beginning to make a happy life for herself in the rocks and tumble weeds of West Texas.

She had dated Johnny on a regular basis since that first date, but it was "nothing serious." She tried to convince her mother he was just a friend and she had no particular special feelings for him, but she lied. She fully expected to have a wonderful time with him on this trip. She was looking forward to getting away by herself – away from her parents' watchful eye. So it was a big disappointment she had not expected when her mother told her the church had asked for volunteers to come along as chaperons. Susie had volunteered.

So, Cali was in a conundrum. She couldn't admit that she was going to have a good time and she couldn't tell her mother she didn't want her to go. But there was not much she could do about it, anyway. Her mother had already agreed. The truth was, Susie Williams wanted and needed to get away, too. This was a perfect opportunity. The getaway was to be from Friday through Sunday. Jim had a gig on Saturday night and a jam session at "Jack's Lounge" on Sunday afternoon. So Susie was also much more excited than she dare let on. She was looking forward to seeing the ocean, too. She had missed the beach as much as Cali, but she was a grown woman and not allowed to express her emotions like Cali. She could hardly wait for the trip to the beach.

"Who are the other chaperons?" Cali wanted to know.

"I think the only other one is Father something-or-other. He is a priest at the Catholic Church organizing the trip. I think he is new there. He is pretty young, just out of seminary."

"His name is Father Francisco Jimenez." Cali interrupted and filled in the blanks of her mother's memory. She immediately realized she had spoken too quickly.

"Hey, that's right, how did you know him?"

After Cali realized she had spoken before she thought, she stammered and hesitated, then dreamed up a quick story on the spur of the moment. "Well, uh, Johnny introduced me to him at the church. You remember. He took me there one night for a church party. He is a really nice man, and very good-looking. Too bad he is a priest. I could really go for him!" Cali was talking fast. She rolled her blue eyes and smacked her lips, purposely over dramatizing. She seemed to know more about the young priest than she wanted anyone to know.

Susie was quite surprised to hear that her daughter already knew this priest -- even more surprised to learn that she had gone to a church for any reason -- even a youth party. She did not recall that Cali had told her about the party, but maybe she forgot. "I just saw him briefly today. He seems like a real nice young man," Susie ignored her daughter's remark. "He asked me to go along since they couldn't get any other parents to volunteer. He said he was anxious to get acquainted with some of the young people here and maybe get some youth groups started. I think he is on a recruiting mission for the Catholic Church." Susie laughed at her own sacrilegious remark.

"Well, he sure won't cause Dad to be jealous. He's probably one of those queer guys. I hear those priests are all queer." Cali's caustic remark restored her sarcastic reputation with her mother. Cali and her parents had never attended a church and Cali had little association with religion of any denomination. They were not atheists; they just had never attended church much since Cali was born.

"I think that is enough, Cali. He certainly won't be interested in me no matter what. Those priests just don't have any interest in women. They aren't allowed to. It's part of their vows. That is the last thing he wants!"

Chapter 14

It's difficult to imagine what it might be like to spend months at a time eating Big Mac's and drinking vodka and living in a doorway. Chui was thinking about this as he ordered the chicken fried steak special at Denny's. He got some mashed potatoes, gravy and some corn. He also told the waitress he wanted a hot roll and a cup of hot, black coffee. He had stayed at the homeless shelter off and on. He loved the meals and the coffee and donuts. It was called *The Lighthouse*. But, they always gave him a big dose of repentance and religion and, although he was raised as a strict catholic, he had long since given up those beliefs and had become an agnostic. So, he didn't go to the shelter often. But he had put up with it sometimes just for the food and warm bed. He was thinking about all this as he was eating his chicken fried steak, mashed potatoes and corn, and drinking his hot coffee. He wanted a drink in the worst way. But he promised the priest. He ordered a refill.

"Boy, do I have a busy day tomorrow," he thought. *"I've got to get some new clothes, some new shoes. And,"* The thought suddenly dawned on him. *"What am I going to do with all this money?"*

Right now it was rolled up in the pocket of his old blue overcoat. He looked at it over the back of the empty chair next to him. He finished the last of his meal, eating the last bite of his dinner roll and chugging down his third cup of coffee. The tab was $12.83, including tax. He ceremoniously laid two dollars on the table for the waitress. He hoped that was enough. He felt a little cheap, seeing as how he had $50,000 in his pocket. He put his overcoat on and walked to the cashier, paid his tab and walked out the door, back towards the Motel 6 next door.

He passed by the glass front door and waved at Punj through the door. He waved back. As he rounded the corner toward room 108, he retrieved the card from his pocket, this time getting it pointed in the right direction. The door opened immediately this time. The sax case was there where he left it. He punched the"ON" button on the remote, bringing the TV to life again. He took all his clean clothes off, except for his underwear, got into bed, pulled up the covers and fell asleep.

The sun was shining through the Venetian blind windows, waking him up. The TV was still on, with the Saturday morning news of El Paso, Texas, and the world. It was to be a beautiful day in West Texas, according to the weather report.

He punched the "0" button on the phone.

"Front desk, this is Punj."

"Hi, Punj, this is Chui in 108."

"Oh yes. What tis it? What can I do fo you, Mistah Vasquez?" His accent was particularly brittle this morning.

"You know a place close by that sells cheap clothes?"

"Let me see. Oh yes. Saint Vincent's Thrift Store. I am sure they would have something you could use. Lots of people donate things. Lots of clothes. Some really expensive. I know you could find something quite satisfactory. It's only a block or so from here."

"They have shoes there?"

"If you can find your size."

'Ok. Thanks. Uh. Oh. Uh. One more thing." Chui hesitated to ask the next question. "Is there a bank that's open on Saturday?" Is there one close to here?"

"Yes. There is a Bank of America branch that's open til noon. But it is about a half mile from here. You need a loan?" It was Punj's futile attempt at humor.

"Oh no – no – Just curious. Just curious, that's all, thank you." He hung up the phone. A blinding flash of the obvious had just occurred to him. "Put the money in a safety deposit box in a bank. It will be safe there. What a great idea." He was happy with his decision. And he had remembered passing by that bank on his way to the motel. He knew right where it was.

He put on his overcoat with the valuable cargo in its pocket, leaving his sax case on the table. He bounded out of his room and passed the glass door again. Punj was busy and did not see him this time. He retraced his route from yesterday and in a few minutes saw the Bank of America in the distance. He arrived and entered.

"Do you have safety deposit boxes here?"

"Sure."

"How much are they?"

"The little ones are $10 for three months."

"I will take a little one. I just have these, uh, papers in a big envelope. Will that fit?"

"I think so." The bank lady was polite and friendly with a Texas drawl.

"Here's the ten." Chui pulled out a ten dollar bill from his pants pocket, left over from the money the priest had left for him. The lady took it and filled out some papers. She asked the usual questions--name, address. He gave her the motel address, which he had memorized for this occasion. He got it from his key card. She gave him the cards to sign and instructed him how to use his key with the bank's key. They went inside the steel vault and she directed him to box number 386. She placed her key in one side and his in the other. The box magically came loose. She pulled it out and handed it to him. She instructed him to place the box back in its slot when he was finished and remove his key. He was to keep his key and she would retrieve hers after he finished his business. She left him alone in the vault. Chui cautiously looked around the vault to see that no one was watching. He slowly pulled the precious envelope out of his pocket and quickly squeezed it into the little box. He was about to snap the box with its contents in the hole in the vault wall, when a sudden panic overtook him. Somehow this did not seem to be the right thing to do. Just as he was about to push the box into the wall, he reached up, yanked out the envelope full of money, rolled it up and placed it back in his overcoat pocket. He pushed the empty safety deposit box back into its nest, pulled out his key, put it on the table and ran out of the bank.

Chapter 15 -- 1950

The Del Rio, Texas, senior class of 1950 had 85 students. Many of them were poor Latinos and could barely afford to buy clothing to go to school. They certainly could not afford to pay $40 for a trip to South Padre Island. And so, there were only 28 students who went on the trip in the spring of 1950. Even though it was a Catholic Church-sponsored trip, it was open to the senior class. It was the creation of the new priest, Father Francisco. Two other parents had indicated they might be able to make the trip and serve as chaperons, but they both backed out at the last minute. They just couldn't afford to get away.

The trip would take them down the U. S. side of the Rio Grande River, through Eagle Pass and on to Laredo and finally into the Rio Grande Valley. They would drive through McAllen, and in and out of all the small towns that form a chain along the U. S. side of the river; towns with names like Mercedes, Weslaco, Alamo, Donna, Pharr, and finally, the biggest city in the valley, Harlingen. This would be the final semblance of civilization until they reached the Gulf of Mexico and South Padre Island. They would need to leave about four a.m. to get there by noon. The trip would take about seven or eight hours.

The sun had crossed the equator on its way back to the northern hemisphere on this twenty-forth day of March of 1950. But it was pitch black dark at 4 a.m. in Del Rio. The yawning seniors all boarded the bus in the dark and promptly fell asleep. The big charter bus made its way down the river and took a turn at Eagle Pass toward Carrizo Springs. It was still dark when it passed through the historical streets of Laredo. But the eastern sun was just peeping across the horizon as things began to turn from the rocky, dusty landscape of west Texas to the hint of green trees and plants. They were getting close to the Rio Grande Valley.

Susie Williams was sitting on the front seat of the bus on the aisle. Her daughter had the window seat next to her. Her mother had insisted that she not sit next to Johnny in the dark bus. Across from Susie on the other aisle was Father Francisco. He had placed a big box of food and supplies and a big cooler full of iced-down drinks in the seat beside him. There were only 28 students and the two chaperons. The bus was not full and everyone had plenty of room.

As the sun crept higher in the early morning sky, Cali opened her eyes and yawned. She looked out the front window of the big bus and nearly came out of her seat. "Palm trees! Look, Momma, palm trees!" She had not called her mother "Momma" for months. It must have slipped out. She would need to watch that. She was showing far too much excitement for the Cali her mother had grown to know but not love too much lately.

Except for the area around San Felipe Park, where the old spring was located in the center of

Del Rio, most of the students had never seen that much abundance of green. Farmers around Del Rio raised lots of onions and some grain. But that was down the river, in the Quemado Valley where there was some irrigation. This was different. Here it was green everywhere. And it got greener as they chugged along highway 83 toward McAllen.

The bus twisted and rocked its way down the highway, through groves of citrus trees and small towns. People were stirring around by now. Pickup trucks made up a majority of the traffic. Rows of furrows were perfectly spaced in the huge fields beside the highway. Each row had cotton plants carefully planted for the harvest in a few months. The high school seniors were pointing and chattering about the new scenery they were witnessing.

McAllen passed, then Weslaco, with its big Tex-Sun citrus juice factory, which provided orange and grapefruit juice all over the world. Finally there was Harlingen, the largest of the Rio Grande Valley cities. The big bus made a right turn in Harlingen onto highway 77 toward Brownsville – then on through beautiful San Benito with its natural Resacas, filled with water like tiny lakes running through the countryside. A final left turn off the Brownsville highway toward Los Fresnos and past a smelly cotton gin waiting for its work to begin in a few weeks. The students were craning their necks to see what new sights might greet them around each curve in the road.

A road sign told them they were headed now toward Port Isabel. Up ahead was a final right curve in the narrow road and, as the bus rounded the curve, everything grew deathly quiet. Everyone, including Cali, Susie and Father Francisco, was rendered speechless for a few seconds. There was the Laguna Madre stretched before them. Padre Island was so far away it could hardly be seen in the distance. The Lagoon looked like a glass-covered mirror. Not a ripple to be seen. "Is that the Gulf?" Someone broke the silence.

The road passed within a few feet of the edge of Laguna Madre Bay. Everyone on the right side of the bus moved to the left to get a better view. "There's some land over there"

"Where?"

"Way over there. See it?"

"That must be Padre Island. Yeah, I can see it now. It's an island way out there!"

At this point South Padre Island is more than a mile from shore and not easily distinguishable. But as the big charter bus rolled down the road beside the water, civilization came closer. Port Isabel was looming in the distance. The undeniable smell of fish and salt water was getting stronger. The small fishing village was teaming with activity this Friday morning. As the senior class peered out the windows of the bus, they could see big fishing yachts moored in the docks and slips along the way. Wealthy Texas businessmen and oilmen kept their fishing boats here. The names and locations of the boats were painted on the sterns. "Houston, New Orleans, Corpus Christi." The young visitors were shouting out the names of the cities. "There is Tampa Bay, Florida!"

As the bus drew nearer to the other end of town there were fishing docks with scores of big shrimp boats bobbing up and down like corks. Each had its name on the bow. "The Mary Bee, Little Paul, Lazy Ann." The names must have been wives, lovers or children. The high school seniors were mesmerized by the new scenery. They could hardly wait to get to where they were going and get out. They had been trapped in the bus for about seven hours.

Up ahead was a small, weather-beaten sign that pointed the way to Padre Island. Between the bus and the island was a very long narrow road, a causeway, just a few feet above the water's surface. The center was raised up like a hump. Small boats could go under without raising the drawbridge. The larger boats needed more room and had to wait for the bridge to be pulled up by its counterweights. There was a tollgate before anyone could begin the journey across the causeway. The bus driver opened the small window and paid the toll. He had been advised and was ready with the proper amount for the busload. Then, the journey across -- something new for virtually all the kids aboard. "It looks like we are driving right on top of the water," someone said. The trip across took only a few minutes and then they were on dry land again. The park where they were to stay was very close to the bridge and it took only five minutes or so to get to the entrance. The bus driver stopped the bus at the gate and got out to make the arrangements. "We have eight cabanas. Is that right?"

"Yes, that is right, both Susie and Father Francisco said in unison.

"OK, let's go."

The bus drove another few hundred feet to the edge of a big concrete slab about the size of three tennis courts with a green mesh tarp over the top and about 25 little cabanas alongside. The bus stopped and 28 kids and two adults piled out as fast as they could and ran toward the slab. Over the edge of the slab the brown sand piled up in windswept dunes with green sea grass growing here and there. It smelled of salt air. About a hundred feet or so down a slight embankment the surf could be heard with its rhythmic pounding and white foam. All the people who had just ridden nearly eight hours, including the two adults, removed their shoes and ran yelling and screaming as fast as they could down the sandy embankment in the soft, warm sand. They splashed into the surf of the Gulf of Mexico, screaming and shouting like they had just been freed from prison. They had finally arrived at South Padre Island.

Chapter 16

St. Vincent's of El Paso was an absolute wonder world of used clothes. There were shirts, pants, suits, sport coats and hundreds of pairs of shoes. And to top it off, Saturday was half-price day. Chui was like a kid in a candy shop. It had been so long since he had bought any clothes, used or otherwise. But after an hour or so, he had managed to find three shirts, three pairs of slacks and a nice sport coat. He also found two pairs of shoes that fit, one brown and one black pair. There were socks and underpants packaged with scotch tape around them in a big box for ten cents each, so he grabbed a handful of those. The bill was just $35, well within his budget. He bundled his clothes up into a big plastic bag donated by the Safeway store, and made his way back to room 108.

This time he went straight to his room, opened the door and dropped the big bag on the bed. He noticed the red light flashing on his phone. "Guess I'd better call Punj and see what it's all about." He picked up the phone and punched the "0." "Punj, this is Chui."

"Yeah I know, I can tell who is calling by which light lights up on this board."

"Why didn't you say so?"

"You never asked. You got a message."

"What do I do?"

"You don't do anything. I'll just read it to you."

"It's from Frank Ortiz."

"Frank Ortiz?"

"Yes, Father Frank Ortiz."

"Oh. What did he want?"

"He just said to remind you to be ready at six. And if you happened to have a pair of dark brown pants, a white shirt and brown coat, that would fit in pretty well. Whatever that all means."

"Thanks. I know what that means." Chui hung up the phone, happy that he had picked out some clothes that fit the situation for tonight. "But there is still this problem with this money. It seems to have given me a headache since I found it. Let's see." He opened his sax case and pulled out the sax and gently laid it on the bed. He looked inside to see if there was a place he could hide the money other than right on top. He remembered a little compartment in the bottom, which was accessible by pulling on a small tab. He had forgotten all about this little place designed to store sheet music or extra reeds, extra neck straps or whatever. He hadn't used it for months. He pulled on the tab and opened up the small space,

which was about half-an-inch thick. It was a
perfect place to lay the envelope. He saw some
papers and coins in the corner. "Wonder what
these are?" He picked the papers up and sorted
through them. "My God, there is my old driver's
license and my passport. I can't believe this. I
must not have looked in this compartment for
quite a while. Shows what happens when you live
on hamburgers and vodka. There are even a
couple of quarters in the corner. I sure could have
used those a time or two." He checked the date on
his license. "I can't believe it's still good. I sure
haven't needed this for a while." Then he opened
his passport and checked it. "Wow, this is still
good for a couple more years." He remembered
getting it a few years ago when he needed to go up
to Canada to do some recording in BC.

"What a perfect place to hide this money.
Then I will know where it is all the time and I can
keep it with me." He reached into the pocket of his
old overcoat and pulled out the envelope, which
had been rolled and twisted. He had tried to
squeeze it into that deposit box at the bank. Then
he poked it into his pocket and carried it around
all day. It needed to be smoothed out a little. He
laid it on the bed and smacked it with the heel of
his hand a few times and got it flat and ready to
stick into the little compartment of his sax case.
He opened it once more and checked the contents.
The money was still there. He smiled. It slid right
in. "Perfecto," he spoke out loud as he pushed
down the flap. He returned the saxophone back to

its rightful place on top of the little compartment
and shut the lid to the case and snapped it closed.

He put the newfound license and passport in
his pocket. "Man, someone is sure looking out for
me. That's all I can say. Maybe that old priest has
something to do with it. What was his name?
Father Frank? Yeah that's it, Frank Ortiz."

After a quick trip over to Denny's for lunch,
he walked back and pushed open the glass door of
the motel lobby. "What time is it, Punj?"

"Two thirty."

"Maybe I had better start getting ready. He
took a leisurely shower and picked out a dark
brown pair of pants and a light yellow shirt. He
didn't get a white shirt, but this would have to do.
He put on his new underwear, brown sox and
shoes. His light brown sport coat was lying on the
bed, ready for action as soon as the priest came to
pick him up.

"These fit pretty good." He looked at
himself in the mirror. "Not a bad-looking
Mexican!" he joked to himself. He wondered who
might have owned these clothes. He thought that
they probably were dead by now. Probably some
rich widow donated them. It was kind of a morbid
thought, but he didn't really care much. He
allowed as how they were long gone now. They
were his clothes now and he was still here, ready to
give these clothes some new life.

Chapter 17

Feldman's liquor store was one of a handful
of businesses on South Padre Island in 1950.
There were two small motels. There was a
Mexican restaurant called the Palmetto Inn.
There was a tiny convenience store known as the
"Sand Box." Then there was a new restaurant and
lounge at the southern tip of the island. This was
quite literally the end of the United States.
Brownsville, Texas, is about ten miles inland from
the Gulf. But Brownsville needed to be an
important port of entry for ocean-going freight.
And so, a deep-water canal was dug through the
sand, right into the city of Brownsville. Huge ships
could wend their way from the Gulf of Mexico past
the south end of Padre Island and into the
Brownsville port between two gigantic walls of
rocks and concrete, which jutted out into the Gulf
about a half mile. These walls of rocks and
concrete were known as the Jetties. Through the
big glass windows of the newly built restaurant,
one could have a cocktail or beer with lunch or
dinner and watch big freighters inch along
through the canal, as though they were traveling
on land. The restaurant was aptly named "The
Jetties Restaurant."

Fourteen boys and sixteen girls from the
senior class at Del Rio High School checked into
their little cabanas for the weekend. This required
seven of the tiny little cabins -- four cabanas for
the girls and three for the boys. Eight had been

rented. There were two chaperons. There was one cabana left. Somehow, someone failed to do the logistics on the sleeping arrangements. Father Francisco and Susie Williams were left to figure out just where they were to bunk down for the night.

There was only one cabana with four bunk beds remaining. Father Francisco stood at the doorway to the remaining shelter and waited for Susie to return from getting all the girls checked into their assigned cabins. "We seem to have a slight logistical problem." He shrugged his shoulders. "There is just this one cabin left for the chaperons."

Susie laughed. "Wouldn't that be just my luck? I have waited for this situation all my life and I get stuck with a priest! I'm only joking, Father. I really think we can be adult about this and just make do. After all, it's just for two nights. I could get my daughter to come and stay with us."

"Now that would be cruel. It's her vacation. She needs to be free to be with her friends and away from her mother." Father Francisco was making sense. "We can leave the door open if you think that will be better. All we are going to do is sleep in here. I am not concerned if you aren't." Susie shrugged her shoulders in agreement.

And so the arrangements were made. Everyone put their bags of shorts and swim suits and other beach clothes and accoutrements in their assigned cabanas and on their assigned bunks, including Susie Williams and Father Francisco Jimenez.

The sun was quickly sinking behind the island on the other side of the Laguna Madre. Everyone had spent the remainder of the afternoon romping on the sand, eating and making the best of every minute of the short time they had to spend playing on the beach. Someone discovered that if they threw up a piece of bread, a flock of seagulls would appear out of nowhere and try to catch it. Except for Cali, these youngsters had never played this game before. It was wonderful. They chased the little crabs and tried to catch them in the sand. They were fascinated by the creatures of the sea.

Someone found some driftwood and part of an old wrecked shrimp boat. They dragged it over and dug a pit and started a nice warm fire at the water's edge. It was a dream evening. The surf was pounding; the cool evening was warmed by sweatshirts and the beach fire. Life was about as good as it gets for this senior class.

Susie and Father had donned some beach clothes themselves. Father Francisco had replaced his white collar and black religious garb with a pair of bright red shorts and a sweatshirt proclaiming "Tulane University" as his Alma Mater. Susie had put on her two-piece swimsuit with an "Eglin Air Base" sweatshirt over the top and yellow shorts over the bottom. She had worn this shirt to the Ft. Walton beach when they lived there. It was appropriate, she thought. They periodically wandered over to the group under the guise of "being sure everyone was OK." Their real mission, however, was to check on the activities. And everyone knew his or her mission. They fooled no one. Cali and Johnny were huddled next to each other. They looked about like Siamese twins. Susie allowed this occasion a bit more latitude than normal. Finally the two chaperons got the message and decided to move a few hundred feet up the beach and let the kids have some fun without their prying eyes. They sat down on a blanket brought from the cabana and began to talk. The surf was easing into a soft and relaxing pulse.

"Do you drink wine?" Father Francisco blurted out this question quite suddenly and unexpectedly.

"Well, yes. We have a glass of wine for dinner quite regularly." Susie answered, rather surprised and a little shocked at the question.

"You know, I have several glasses of wine every day," the priest quipped. "I have grown to love wine. I really like red wine -- especially cabernet. Of course, the church doesn't provide such good wine so I have to buy my own. I drink wine at all the masses I say." He stared out over the vast Gulf for a moment. "Some of us get to be alcoholics!" He laughed at his unexpected truism. "Would you like a glass of wine?"

"Right now? Right here. On the beach"

"Sure. I saw a liquor store up there on the road. We could slip away and get a bottle and get back before anyone knew we were gone. We might as well enjoy this trip, too." The priest was not sounding like a man of the cloth at all. But he was easily convincing Susie. Jim would be playing a gig tomorrow night and would be gone all Sunday afternoon at a jam session at Jack's lounge. He had a chance to have his outlet and have some fun and she was cooped up in that damn little trailer. All these thoughts were racing at the speed of light through her brain as she composed her response to Father Francisco's suggestion.

"I think that would be a marvelous idea. Let's do it!" She let her thoughts go out through her mouth. The prospect of a glass of wine on the beach with a very good-looking, bright young man, with the surf in the background and some good conversation, sounded like one of the best suggestions she had heard in a long time.

Feldman's Liquor Store was about a half mile up the beach on the road that traverses the center of the island. It was an easy walk for the two adults, both of whom were in great physical condition. Not more than ten minutes later, they had purchased three bottles of cabernet, two wine glasses and a corkscrew. It was another ten-minute walk back to the beach. Susie clung onto the priest's arm as they made their way back in the dark through the sand dunes. The glass bottles clanged together in the paper bag as they carried them down the sandy beach back to their beach blanket.

They could see the bonfire blazing away and kids around the fire doing whatever kids do. Someone's radio was playing 1950 hits of the day.

"They didn't even know we were gone." Father Francisco, never having had teenagers, was probably a bit naive. Susie wanted to correct his naiveté but decided to let him think the best.

"I am sure you are right," she lied.

He swiftly made short work of the cork in the first bottle. The cork made a "pop" sound as it came out in one quick pull. There was not much need for allowing the wine to "breathe." It was not exactly a top-of-the-line winery. But it would serve tonight's purpose. The purple liquid splashed into each glass and the glasses touched each other in an obligatory toast. The wine was not expensive, but it tasted so very good to Susie. She sipped on the glass again and again, faster than she should, she knew. But she loved the quick relaxation she could feel coming over her mind and her body.

They talked about philosophy and literature. They discussed everything from religious history to the weather. Susie had not had such a delightful experience for years. Father Francisco poured her

another glass, as a good host would. It was such a
wonderful night. She wanted it to last forever and
another glass of wine might just keep it going a
little longer. She leaned back on her elbows and
looked up at the starry sky above the gulf. The
surf was making such a wonderfully rhythmic
sound. Time was rushing along much too fast for
her.

The second bottle of wine popped and she
heard her glass being filled again. The sky was
spinning, but she didn't care. She laughed like she
had not laughed for months. Father Francisco
scooted closer in the night chill. She didn't object.

Chapter 18

Chui was ready to go about 5:30 -- half an hour ahead of time. He darted out the door of his room and up to the lobby. He swung open the door but no one was at the counter. He walked up and looked behind and all around and still saw no one. He felt like a member of the family by this time. After all, Punj had washed his clothes and given him a razor, a toothbrush and even acted as his valet. He had given him a robe from the Chicago Hilton and collected money for him from the priest and taken his messages. He needed one more thing. "Punj -- Punj," he yelled behind the counter toward the back room where Punj lived in his apartment.

"What tis it?" A voice came from way in the back of the hotel office. "What tis it?" The voice came closer.

"I forgot to get any cologne or deodorant. Do you have some I can have?"

Punj drew a big breath and sighed and rolled his eyes. "OK. OK. Just a moment." He went back to his little apartment and retrieved some Old Spice deodorant and shaving lotion and handed them to Chui. "I wouldn't let just anyone use my private stuff. Just use it here and give it back to me, OK?"

"Oh, sure." He slapped some lotion on his clean-shaven face and unbuttoned his shirt and squirted some spray under each arm. He handed it back and said, "I don't care if you are a Hindu, you are still a great guy." They both laughed.

He returned to his room and a few minutes later there was a knock on his door. He put on his new sport coat, grabbed his saxophone and opened the door. Standing there in a sport coat and white shirt was an old man with snow-white hair and a white beard. "You ready?"

"Are you? You look different."

"I don't wear my priest suit when I play a gig. Most people don't even know I am a priest. I am just Frank -- Just Frank, the piano man. OK. You ready? Let's head for the border?"

Chapter 19

"I see more students than we brought with us." Susie seemed not terribly concerned with this discovery. She had grown a little giggly and was slurring her words ever so slightly. She had sipped down three glasses of wine and was feeling the results.

Father Francisco focused his attention towards the blazing fire and began to count heads as best he could. He stood up and walked a few steps closer to get a better view. He nodded his head as he counted each student. He returned and sat down next to Susie, a little closer than he was before. "I count thirty two," he reported. "If my math is correct, that is about four more than we brought. I think someone joined the party. I guess that is OK as long as there is no trouble."

"As long as there is no trouble," Susie parroted his words. She was just pouring herself a fourth glass of wine. "Let them have a good time. Those extra people are probably some teenagers who are here from some other school. I think it's good for them to get to know other kids from other places." Susie was having a bit of difficulty getting her words to come out like she wanted. And besides, she was having such a great time with Father Francisco; she really didn't want to be bothered with the responsibility of policing teenagers. Father Francisco pulled their blanket up around them and snuggled up a little closer to her. It was beginning to get cool and they had no fire to keep them warm.

"I want to know about you." She turned her head toward him. "Where did you come from? What brought you to Del Rio?"

"Why did you become a priest?" They both spoke that question in unison.

"You are making fun of me." Susie feigned a pout and laughed.

"Everyone wants to know the answer to that question. Well, I will tell you all I know about that. I was educated at a very strict Jesuit school. I was in a gifted group. God was good to me – gave me a good brain and a talent for music. I finished private school at fourteen. I went on to Tulane and got pretty wrapped up in music and religion. I thought I could contribute to the world better as a priest. I have to admit; I had a little help with my decision from the Jesuits. But it sounded like a good way to live my life. I finished seminary and was ordained last year. Then, at the ripe old age of twenty-two, they sent me to Del Rio and here I am. Not very glamorous, is it?"

"What do you play? I mean what musical instrument?"

"Piano. I play jazz piano. It was a great diversion. I played at clubs in New Orleans during school. I still play when I get the chance."

"My husband is a musician. He plays the piano and trumpet."

"Yes I know."

"I wouldn't ask this question if I hadn't had a few glasses of wine. But are you... I mean -- Uh --"

"No, I am not."

"What did you think I was going to ask?"

"Am I a homosexual?"

"How did you know?"

"Because, frankly, a few of us are. It's a fair question. But I am a normal heterosexual, red-blooded American boy. But I am about to freeze. Could we get a little closer and keep each other warm?" He poured yet another glass of wine for each of them and they touched their bodies together in the dark and drank their wine. Susie knew what she was feeling was not quite right, but the wine erased the guilt.

The four young strangers who joined the group that was gathered around the fire brought some exciting new conversation to the unsophisticated Del Rio High School seniors. They brought some new friendships. And they brought something else. They brought some stuff from

Mexico. It looked like ground-up weeds. That is because it *was* ground-up weeds. It was called marijuana. They were showing the curious students just how to roll it up in some cigarette papers and light it, pass it around and smoke it.

And so, as the chaperons were having their next glass of wine and wondering what was going to happen next in the dark of night while they huddled together to keep warm beside the Gulf of Mexico, their charges were sitting around the fire down the beach getting high on grass.

Chapter 20

When the Base Commander calls you to come into his office it is either really good news or really bad news. Col. John Bainbridge had been assigned to Laughlin Air Force Base to get it organized and up and running. Hundreds of young pilots were on their way. Each one was already a trained pilot, but only in "prop" aircraft. They had been trained as pilots, but none had been behind the stick of a jet fighter. That was the mission of this base. Each one would climb aboard a T-33 trainer, along with a flight instructor, and learn to fly very fast and very close. They would be our future fighter pilots. Each day would begin with a military style march down to the flight line, where they would conduct a pre-flight meeting, climb aboard their jets and take off into the wild blue yonder. They would return and land in the afternoon, get into marching formation and march back to their officer's quarters for some study and relaxation.

This Friday afternoon was especially lonely. Susie and Cali were gone for the weekend to South Padre Island and he didn't have anything to do until tomorrow night at the NCO club. The message had been delivered to his office in the base theater by an aide from the Base Commander's office. "To: Msgt James Williams. From: Office of the Base Comdr, Subj, Meeting at 1400 hours, Fri. Msg: Please meet with Colonel James Bainbridge at 1400 hours, Friday, 24 Mar, 1950.

The military always used abbreviations whenever possible. Jim was not only curious, but also a little apprehensive about the meaning of this note. He checked his shoes and put on his tie. He checked himself in the reflection of the theater show card glass and headed for Headquarters.

"I have an appointment with Colonel Bainbridge," Sgt. Williams stiffly saluted the Second Lieutenant sitting at the desk outside the door marked "Commander."

"Let's see. Oh, here it is. Sgt. James Williams?"

"Yes sir."

"OK -- just a second, Sarge. The Lieutenant disappeared behind the door and spoke quietly to the man seated behind the big desk, then returned. "Col. Bainbridge will see you now."

Anyone who has been an enlisted man in the military has been brainwashed since basic training. They instinctively know that anyone who wears the rank of an officer on his collar is to be treated with the utmost respect, whether they deserve it or not. And, furthermore, if that symbol of brass goes up the echelon to a Captain, Major, Lt. Colonel, Colonel and on up to General, the degree of respect and fear of screwing up increases exponentially. And so -- here is Master Sgt. Jim Williams, standing in front of a full bird Colonel, the Base Commander. He is the head of this entire installation. No one can tell him what to do or order him around. Even other Colonels under his command do what he says. All these thoughts were flashing through Jim's head as he clicked his heels and saluted smartly in front of the Colonel's desk. "Sergeant James Williams reporting, Sir!" Jim spit out the words in his best militaristic manner.

He had no idea what to expect. He had never met the Commander personally. He had seen him at the Officer's Club when his band was playing there. But he had not mixed with any of the officers, he wasn't really allowed to. He had heard that the commander was a pretty fair sort of guy and a reasonable man. But Jim had no idea what the Colonel wanted with him. He had not done anything wrong that he could recall. Did he have too many beers at Jack's? Maybe he wasn't supposed to play off the base? Maybe he charged too much to play at the Officer's or NCO Club? These hundreds of thoughts were racing through the neurons.

"Sit down, Jim."

"Yes, Sir." The Commander called him by his name instead of his rank. That was a good start.

"I understand you have some knowledge of music?" He had an open folder in front of him. He looked down briefly and then back at Jim. "I have heard you play at the Officer's Club. I played a little trumpet myself back in college, not nearly as good as you, but we had a little combo back in Illinois."

"My God, this was going good. He is really a nice guy. Nothing like I expected," Jim was thinking. "Well, thank you, sir. I didn't know you, uh, you just didn't –"

"Seem like the type to be a musician?" The Colonel finished Jim's sentence and laughed as he leaned back in his big chair.

Jim laughed, too. "Well, as a matter of fact, Uh, Yes. Uh, Yes, Sir."

"He seems so – well – human," Jim thought as he focused on the myriad of medals and honors pinned to his chest. He had a big set of wings above his pocket. This meant he was a "rated" officer, a trained combat pilot. Jim began to relax a little. But he still wondered what the hell the Base Commander wanted. He surely didn't call him in to talk about music or his college days at the U of I. Or maybe he did. *"He could call anyone in to talk about anything he wanted to talk about."* Jim mused at his thoughts.

"Jim, as you know, we are going to have hundreds of young cadets in here real soon. Some are already here. They will be here from all over the free world. We are getting them from France, South Korea, Germany, England, and places I can't even remember right now. But most will be from the good ole U S of A." The Colonel leaned forward toward Jim as if to become more serious. "Training Command HQ has told me that we can have a small band if we want one. And I want one." He became more animated as he proceeded to explain. "We need to be able to march these cadets around the base in a military manner, and to play for graduation ceremonies – things like that. And we need to have a band to play for their formal affairs. After graduation they will greet my staff and me at a formal party. We need some nice background music for this kind of stuff. They have told me that I have the authority to begin to select people from my own base to form the band until we can get in the pipeline for more musicians from other sources. We can have up to twenty musicians. I would like to start with a nucleus of guys from here. What do you think?"

Jim could hardly believe what he was hearing. All he could get out of his mouth was, "Wow. That is terrific, Colonel Bainbridge." Jim had never called him anything but "Sir." Saying his name out loud sounded good and rather natural to him. It was Jim's turn to get excited and animated. "We have several guys who would qualify. Some of them play in my little band already."

"Yes, I know. That's why you are sitting here in front of me right now. Jim, I want you to get together a list of guys who would qualify. You can have access to the personnel files. You can audition them to see if they are good enough.

Remember, they will need to play military music as well as big band, dance music. These men will need to be Jacks-of-all-trades, so to speak. I can probably get four or five from other bases here in Texas right away, but that's about all right now. I can get some instruments real quick. We can requisition some from local music stores or even over in San Antonio. But we need to get started yesterday."

Jim was so excited he could hardly contain himself. "Yes Sir. Yes Sir, Colonel."

"A couple more things. We will get all your AFPC numbers changed to reflect 'Bandsman.' That means it will be your full duty assignment – no additional duties. And one other thing, we need a bandleader. He will be given a rank of Warrant Officer, making him a fully ranked officer in the US Air Force." The Colonel reached in his desk drawer and fished out a box with two bars in it and opened it toward Jim. He handed it across the desk. "What do you think of that idea, Warrant Officer Williams?"

Chapter 21

The sunrise over the Gulf of Mexico east of Padre Island is just as spectacular as the sunset. But, often most people don't get to see it. They are not yet awake. The door to the cabana, which housed Susie Williams and Father Francisco, remained open, as promised.

The cabin faced the east and the sun blasted right into the interior of the little quarters. "Oh, my God, what did I do to myself?" Susie rubbed her head and tried to focus her eyes. She was sleeping on the top bunk above the priest. She still had on her swimsuit with the sweatshirt and yellow shorts. She was covered up with the blankets that came with the cabin. "I think I need some coffee really bad."

The priest was sitting up on the side of his bunk. He had already been up for a short while and had managed to heat up some water on the little camp stove he had brought along. He put some instant coffee in a paper cup and poured the water over it. He stirred it up and handed it to Susie. "Here, this ought to help. It's pretty strong."

"Father? I wish I could call you something besides Father. That sounds so formal. And besides, I am not a Catholic and you are not my Father." She managed a little chuckle.

"Well, I guess you don't remember last night? You decided I would be 'Francis.' So that sounds fine to me. After all, I am a few years younger than you. I think we should just get along with the day. Last night was wonderful. We had a great time. But it's a new day and we have 28 kids to feed."

"My God, Father, I don't remember last night very well."

"Maybe it's just as well. How's your head?"

Susie sipped her coffee. "Getting better. Thanks for the coffee. Is that Jetties restaurant open?"

"I don't know but we can go take a look. It's right down the road."

Susie hopped down from her bunk and kept the blanket around her. Father Francisco politely left the little cabin and closed the door so Susie could have a little privacy. She snatched her little night case and her small suitcase and headed for the big public restroom about 25 feet down the way. She found the women's half, went in and got herself ready for whatever the day brought forth.

Father Francisco did a similar thing in the men's bathhouse.

It was a beautiful morning. None of the students was stirring. There was a big hole in the sand just over the dunes on the beach. It was full of black ashes. A couple of towels and some bottles and paper cups were strewn around. The fire had gone out long ago. Off in the distance, some dark clouds were forming and the breeze was blowing from the sea. It looked as though the beautiful sunshine might not last all day.

Susie reappeared at the door of the cabin. She still had on her yellow shorts and a different sweatshirt. The sweatshirt proclaimed she belonged to the "U S Air Force." Father Francisco had already arrived from the men's shower room. He had donned his red shorts, again, and his "Tulane" sweatshirt. He had on sandals and no socks.

"Maybe we could run over to that Jetties restaurant and see if they have some real coffee." Susie was obviously desperate for some "real" coffee.

"OK. Sounds good to me."

The two chaperons trekked across the big concrete slab and walked the few hundred yards toward the big sign that identified the Jetties. It was open. On weekends, lots of early morning fishermen stopped there for an early breakfast before setting out for the day. The new restaurant had a large dining area with big picture windows all around so patrons could enjoy a view of the Gulf and the jetties from nearly anywhere in the restaurant. The bar was a smaller room with tables and a small dance floor. There was a small spinet piano. Susie and the priest each ordered a large paper cup of hot coffee. They paid and walked back to their temporary home.

Father Francisco had brought supplies for breakfast and lunch. The students were expected to have enough money to buy some of their own food. The priest thought maybe they might all go to the Jetties tonight. He had seen the piano in the restaurant. He thought he might have a little surprise for them on this Saturday night.

The Coleman camp stove was set up on a picnic table out on the pavilion under the canopy. Father Francisco had pumped up the gas tank, making a nice hot fire to cook some Ole Buckwheat pancakes. He had brought all the ingredients in a cooler. The ice was nearly melted by now, but it was still cold enough. The Sand Box was a short distance away and they had plenty of ice for sale. He had a big gallon glass jar into which he dumped the powder, milk and eggs. He shook it vigorously.

"You are quite a chef." Susie complimented him.

"You get to be a good cook when you have to cook for yourself. Either that or you starve." He put two skillets on the stove and put some oil in each one. The students were beginning to wander out of their little quarters by now. A big stack of paper plates was on the table, along with some butter and a big jug of Log Cabin syrup. He poured some batter in each skillet and began to cook some breakfast for the sleepy-eyed kids. "You need to eat with your fingers. This ain't the Hilton." The students grabbed the pancakes as he stacked them on a plate. Susie stood beside him and passed out the butter and syrup. There was also a stack of paper cups and several jugs of orange juice. Susie poured and distributed the Saturday morning breakfast. Thunder could be heard in the eastern sky over the Gulf.

Chapter 22

"Club One." That was the neon sign over the big restaurant, lounge and nightclub about a mile across the international bridge in Mexico. That is where Frank and Chui parked their car and got out. Chui grabbed his sax case out of the back seat and followed Frank through the door. It was dark by now. The lights of Juarez had begun to light up the streets. Inside, it was dim and smoky. The two made their way toward the small stage. "Chui, this is Kiki. He is the best drummer in Mexico." A black man with a beard and glasses turned and stuck out his hand.

"Buenos noches, mon." Kiki had a Jamaican dialect.

"And this is Rubin, the bone man." Ruben looked to be Hispanic.

"Hey man. Que paso? What's the haps?" Rubin was a tall skinny nervous guy. "Frank said you blow some decent sax. I can't wait to hear you play, man."

"Well, that will happen pretty soon. It's nearly 8. Let's get started."

Chui did not forget what was in his sax case other than his saxophone. He carefully placed the case on the little bandstand so he could see it. He leaned it up against the piano next to the wall. "*No one could get this out of here unless they came up on the stand and walked through the musicians.*" Chui felt confident it was safe.

After some "noodling" around and tuning up for a few minutes, Frank sat down and cracked his knuckles a couple of times. He turned to Chui. "What do you want to start with?"

"Whatever you usually do," Chui shrugged his shoulders. He appreciated the offer, but he didn't feel it was his place to suggest the first tune. He would leave that to someone else for now.

"We don't really have any theme song. We just pick something and go. How about 'Lady is a Tramp in F'? We'll play an ensemble, then, Chui, since you are the newest, you can take two. Rube is next. Then I will play a couple. Then we will trade fours with Kiki for a couple. I will signal for two and out." These quick instructions from the piano man set the pattern for the first and most of the other tunes to be played that night at Club One.

Chui had longed for this perfect scenario. They all appeared to be really good musicians. The club seemed to allow the band to play pretty much what they wanted. And the first tune was something he knew really well. You couldn't beat that.

Frank played eight bars of wonderful chords as he and Kiki set the rhythm. Chui knew this was going to be a great night right from that first note. Kiki laid down the beat with some brushes and high hat cymbals in the background. The first note was heaven for Chui. Rube hit it, too, with a perfect unison chorus. They played it through twice and on the last two measures, that glorious silence which gave Chui the kick off he needed to start his own solo eight beats early. It was like someone blasted him off with a rocket. His fingers flew for the eight beats left to him to play all alone with no sound whatsoever. Then on the first downbeat, Kiki and Frank hit it on the button and Chui about peed his pants as he closed his eyes and went into his solo chorus. He could not miss. Frank's chords were leading him like runway lights guiding an airliner. He had gone to heaven for a few short minutes. His heart was beating double time.

Chui finished his two times through and wanted to play on but his turn was over for now. He stopped eight beats early and gave Rube the same kickoff on his trombone chorus that he had been afforded. Rubin played fantastically. He had, obviously, played professionally for many years. He added some nice lip slurs and wonderful improvising--nothing terribly complicated, just simple and tasty. He made it sound easy.

The fours gave each musician a chance to show off for four bars and then another chance as the "trading fours" with Kiki continuing twice through. He played quietly, but with the rudiments of an accomplished drummer. His four bar solos were not flashy, just nice and precise.

Then -- the final chorus. Each man was lost in his own world with his own special rendition. And, yet, each musician fitted his improvisation into the precise chord structure designed by the composer. Chui was transfixed. Then the final note, strung out until Kiki's final beat. All stopped at the exact same moment. Four musicians, who had never played together, who had not even met Chui until tonight; and all starting and stopping and playing as though they had been together since birth. Chills went up Chui's neck as the last note went silent for a second or two. "This is living. This is what it is all about. Where have I been for the past few years?" Chui was a happy cat.

Chapter 23

It was just past noon at South Padre Island in March of 1950. The youngsters had eaten their pancakes and drunk their orange juice. Some were romping on the beach, feeding the gulls. Some were sitting around on the pavilion, under the green canopy, talking and "horsing around." Father Francisco was down on the beach with his red shorts and sweatshirt, cleaning up some of the mess from the night before. Susie Williams stayed at the pavilion. They purposely separated themselves from each other. Cali was walking on the beach with Johnny.

Big black clouds were beginning to move onto the beach from the Gulf. The wind began to blow and one could hear thunder in the distance. The open beach is not a good place to be during an electrical storm. Both the priest and Susie knew that their beach time might be short lived. As the sun was dampened by the clouds, the rain started to fall in sprinkles at first, then in bigger and heavier drops. The clouds formed fog and mist, making it difficult to see more than a few hundred feet. The rain was now falling in sheets, catapulted across the beach by the wind gusts. The two chaperons separately made the same decision. They called the students onto the concrete slab, under the canopy, which provided them with some shelter from the rain.

"I think we need to go somewhere where it is warm and dry," Father Francisco proclaimed to the group. Susie agreed. "I am sure that restaurant over there would love to have us come in and keep them company." Everyone quickly agreed with that suggestion. The weather was getting nasty and cold. They each grabbed a jacket or sweat shirt and ran in a group toward the Jetties Restaurant.

The Texas hospitality was evident as the group of thirty people filed into the Jetties, stomping their feet and shaking out their wet clothes. "Y'all look like a real nice bunch of kids." The waitress greeted them with her Texas drawl. The restaurant was empty. "This weather sure puts a damper on things, don't it? Well, y'all make yourselves to home and maybe the rain'll blow over. It usually don't last long." She was trying to be optimistic.

Father Francisco had slipped over to the piano and sat down on the bench. "I have a surprise for you," he shouted. "We will have some special entertainment today." He hit a few chords and the group looked toward him, wondering what might be next. He tinkled the keys with a brief introduction and began a great impersonation of Nat King Cole and "Route 66."

"I didn't know he could play the piano. Wow, he is good." The students were obviously surprised and delighted.

"He sounds just like Nat King Cole."

The priest, in his red shorts and sweat shirt, called on some of the students to come up and gather around him. They did. He played some other King Cole songs. He played Vaughn Monroe and did a rendition of "Racing with Moon." He belted out a good rendition of Billy Eckstein and "I Apologize." They joined in when he played and sang, "They Tried to Tell Us We're Too Young."

They ate hamburgers and hot dogs and drank cokes. They jitterbugged to "Orange Colored Sky," as he imitated Frankie Laine. "You are wonderful!" Susie Williams sat down beside him on the bench. She whispered with her mouth very close to his ear as he played on. He wanted to respond but thought better of it.

Cali and Johnny danced very close together as he played "Nature Boy." Susie swirled around and nodded toward them and they loosened up a little. Cali passed by her mother and spoke into her ear through her clenched teeth. "Maybe you shouldn't be so critical, Mother!" Susie pretended she didn't know what she was talking about, but she did. She got up from her seat beside the priest and Cali sat down in her place. "Maybe I had better sit here and let you go check on the dancers to be sure they aren't getting too close together." Cali put on her best phony smile as she spoke those sarcastic words to her mother.

Susie Williams wondered just how much her daughter knew. *"Maybe she knows more than I know."* She tried to find some humor in the situation.

Johnny stood on the perimeter watching his girlfriend sitting next to the star of the show, swaying back and forth with the music and putting her head on his shoulder as she laughed at his antics. She "accidentally" would rub her bare leg against Father Francisco's bare leg as she swayed to his music. She glanced toward the group once in awhile and watched as her mother worked her way to the edge of the group. She could detect a forced smile on her mother's face. She had hit a nerve and her mother did not yet know if it was on purpose or just a guess.

The afternoon storm had begun to let up. The priest had been performing for about two hours. He was about out of gas. The kids were beginning to stop singing along and had started to look out the big picture windows toward the beach. "Look. There is a big ship!" A huge freighter was entering the canal on its way toward the Brownsville port. It looked like it was close enough to touch. The students ran out the door toward the jetties and began to wave and shout at the seamen on the deck of the big ship. They were thrilled when they all waved back and began to shout at them. They couldn't understand what they were saying. The name on the ship was Italian and so was the language they were hearing. The few students who spoke Spanish were able to translate some of the comments. "The two languages are similar," they explained to the others.

Father Francisco raised his hands and squeezed his fingers into fists and then straightened them. He did this several times. His hands were obviously tired from the two-hour concert. Cali was still seated beside him. She gave him a quick kiss on the cheek and told him how much the group appreciated his efforts today. He pulled away but only slightly. He was obviously pleased with this show of gratitude from such a beautiful blond haired young woman. Johnny had gone outside with the group to wave at the ship. Susie was standing at the window ostensibly watching the ship but could readily see the piano and the two seated at it in the window's reflection. She could watch her daughter and the young priest without their knowledge. Their bare legs were touching, again. It couldn't be accidental this time. She wondered what the hell was going on and why.

Chapter 24

The Soviet Union, throwing another ember on the cold war tinderbox, had begun to provide North Korea with arms and training. The North Korean army was advancing toward the South and about to take over the entire peninsula. The United States, in 1950, had chosen to protect the South Korean people by sending vast numbers of armed forces and equipment to fight off the northern invasion. It was to be called a "conflict" and not a "war." The Selective Service required all men at age eighteen to register for the draft. Some few men chose to ignore this call to arms for their country. But, the vast majority of young men answered the call and were summoned by a lottery system governed by each county in the United States. Val Verde County, Texas, was ready with its monthly lottery numbers. Each young man over eighteen years of age held his breath until he heard the results of this drawing. Twenty-three-year-old Ramon Vasquez got the call. His number was pulled out of the hat. He was about to be drafted into the army infantry.

Paco was not sure how he felt about that. He was proud that he had a son to give. But he was, naturally, concerned about his son's welfare lest he get sent to Korea and combat duty. Ramon was resigned to his fate. But Damon, who was about two minutes younger than his brother, decided it was not good for them to be separated in this manner. Neither man was married, so there was no wife or child to be considered. But, they had been together their entire lives, working on and running the huge ranch. They were identical twins and few could tell them apart.

Damon had a plan. He made an appeal to his father to contact the draft board and see if both of them might be able to join the Marine Corps together instead of having Ramon go through the Selective Service system. Paco talked it over with his wife and pondered about it a lot. He was very proud of both of his sons for making this decision. He called Ester Tijeras, the chairwoman of the Val Verde County Selective Service board. He had known her since high school and was able to speak frankly. She told him it was normally a given that whoever was drawn would be taken into the Army. However, because of the circumstances of the situation, she would pull a string or two and allow the boys to join the Marines together.

Ester thought it was a great chance to get her picture in the local newspaper. She contacted Charley Chavez, the city desk editor. He saw it as a terrific story. "Local twins join Marines." He created the headline instantly in his mind. The Marine recruiter was ecstatic. He got two new recruits and a big newspaper story without lifting a finger. And so it was. In the spring of 1950, Ramon and Damon Vasquez signed up together and were accepted and shipped off to California for basic training in the U S Marine Corps.

That night, Paco Vasquez, the big macho man, the owner of the big Iturria Ranch just north of Del Rio, Texas, silently, privately and secretly cried himself to sleep.

Chapter 25

"Hey, the sun is about to set!" Susie thought up a good excuse to break up the intimate conversation between her daughter and the young priest. They quickly jumped up from the piano bench as though they had been caught doing something wrong. "What say we all walk over to the other side of the island and watch the sunset over the bay?" Without waiting for an answer, she opened the door facing the beach and shouted at the other students who had joined in with a couple of Australians throwing a boomerang and trying to catch it. The weather had cleared up and the clouds had moved inland, setting the stage for a gorgeous sunset. Susie didn't really care that much about sunsets, but this was a great excuse to get Cali back to "normal." She had been sitting on the piano bench talking to Father Francisco for about ten minutes since he had stopped playing. They were involved in a very intense conversation about something. Susie had been watching them in the reflection in the glass window, as she appeared to be looking outside. She wondered what this emotion was she was feeling. Was she jealous? Of whom? Yes, she had a wonderful time with the priest the previous night. But some of that was pretty foggy after all the wine she had consumed. She didn't even remember going to bed. But she didn't remember doing anything terribly wrong. Why was Cali so engrossed in conversation with this priest? Were they talking about her? Did she do something she didn't remember?

"Let's go, Mom!" Cali grabbed her arm and broke her train of thought. "The sunset won't wait for us."

It was about a ten-minute walk across the island to the "Bay Side." There was a small marina with a few small boats moored in the slips. A fueling station was there with a long gasoline hose laying coiled up on the pier. The group of seniors gathered on the dock and watched the sun "sink slowly in the west." The causeway became only a silhouette. It looked like a snake hovering above the red water. The sun reflected itself in the glassy waters of Laguna Madre Bay. It was spectacular!

This was the last night out for this group of Del Rio High School seniors. They would be leaving before sunrise tomorrow, headed back home. They each had a lot to tell their families. Susie hoped that Cali wouldn't tell everything she seemed to know. Susie was suddenly very sad. She knew something was happening that she couldn't explain. She had this motherly intuition that Cali was, somehow, different than she was when they arrived two days ago. She didn't understand what was going on. Everything seemed to be out of her control. She began to think about Jim. She wished she were back home. She wished she hadn't come at all. It was dark and no one could see the tears on her cheeks, as she stood alone. The sun disappeared over Port Isabel.

Chapter 26

The night was far too short for Chui Vasquez. He kept his saxophone connected to the neck strap around his neck, as he shook hands with Kiki and Rube. "Man, that was fabulous!" They had played four hours, but it seemed like four minutes. He wanted it to go on, but the time was up. The music ran the gamut -- from that first tune through a lot of Latin rhythms -- and old standards and even some quasi rock and roll. Chui had never played some of the tunes, but he let Frank do a piano solo or he joined in, noodled around or just followed the chords and faked it. He had learned to fake it pretty well when necessary. Every song was not played perfectly, but they were certainly acceptable. He finally, reluctantly, got his sax case out from behind the piano and opened it up. He quickly checked the little compartment in the bottom. The envelope was still there. He knew it would be. He carefully removed the neck and mouthpiece from the instrument and placed it in its little nest inside the case. His neck strap went into the corner compartment. He carefully placed his saxophone in the case and closed the case. He hoped he would have a chance to open it again and play with this group real soon.

"Hey, mon, that was a blast!" Kiki was offering his hand. Again, Chui shook it vigorously. "Hope we can do it again real soon."

"Yeah, me too. I had such a ball. You guys are so good. Man, I just can't express how wired I am right now."

Rubin came over after he had put his trombone in its case. "You blow better than Frank said. I loved those riffs we got into on some of that Latin stuff." Rube was shaking his right hand and patting him on the back with his left hand at the same time.

"Man, oh man. We did some good stuff, didn't we? And you play so tasty and mellow. I loved it." Chui returned the compliment.

Frank had gone over to the club manager and collected the money. He peeled off twenty dollar bills to each man. He gave Chui seven twenties, $140. He had no idea what the other guys got. He didn't care. He didn't care if he got paid at all. He was walking on air right now.

He put his sax case in the back seat of Frank's car and climbed in and headed for the U S border and the International Bridge toward El Paso. Both men were quiet for a while. The line across the bridge was not too long tonight. It took only about twenty minutes to get to the customs agent. "I need you to pull over into this inspection area." The young guard seemed to need to do more than the usual cursory check.

"Now, what the hell?" Frank spoke to Chui out of the side of his mouth. "It must be one of

117

those random checks. They do that once in awhile. I got caught in one a couple of years ago. It shouldn't take long."

"Just get out and let me have a look in your car." The customs guard was trying to be polite, without much success.

The two men got out. Frank's nationality was, obviously Hispanic. Chui certainly looked the part, also.

"You both U S citizens?"

"Yes sir. Here is my passport." Frank produced his and handed it to the guard. "Chui, do you have some ID?"

"As a matter of fact, I do." Chui thanked whatever Gods may be for finding his lost passport earlier in the day. He reached into his pocket and produced it. "Shouldn't that take care of it?" He whispered to Frank.

"I hope so."

"OK, but I need to take a look in the car." The zealous agent opened the back door and saw the saxophone case lying in the seat. "What's in there?"

"That is his saxophone. We have been playing at Club One tonight and that is his musical instrument." Frank jumped in with the detailed explanation. Chui was happy to let him handle it.

"Well, open it up and let me have a look."

Chui's skin went cold. *"How the hell am I going to explain that $50,000 in there?"* His brain was struggling with this unexpected scenario. He nearly panicked.

"Officer, I know I don't look the part right now, but I am a priest. In addition to my regular church duties, I have a small band and we play over in Mexico now and then. This man is a member of my band. He is a musician. He plays the saxophone. We are both US citizens, as you can see. I know you are just doing your job, but I would appreciate a little special consideration."

"Just open the saxophone case and let me have a look!"

Chui unhooked the two clasps. He popped open the top. The agent got out his flashlight and stuck his head into the back seat of the car to get a better look. He poked around in the corners and opened up the small compartment where the neck strap and reeds were kept. Chui held his breath and tried to act calm but his heart was beating double time. *"If he opens that bottom, I am a dead man."* He took a deep breath.

The man pulled his body out of the car and put away his flashlight. "OK, Father. Sorry for the delay. Just routine. You understand?"

"Yes, my son. I understand. Bless you." Frank genuflected toward the agent. He nodded in appreciation.

Chui was sweating like it was July and it was barely spring. They pulled out of the little stall and made their way into El Paso and on to the motel. "How did he know you *really* were a priest?" Chui let out a long breath of air.

Frank threw his passport over to Chui. "I had my picture taken with my collar on. Wasn't that clever of me?" He chuckled. Chui looked at the picture of a distinguished looking priest on the document. He also noticed the full name. "Francisco Ortiz y Jimenez."

The Motel 6 was dark. It was after midnight. Chui got out of the car, snatched his sax out of the back seat and stuck his head in the window. "Frank, I can't tell you how much I enjoyed this night. I hope we can do it again soon. You have saved my life."

"Don't get maudlin on me. You did a great job tonight. I knew you would. You are a fine musician. I will be in touch. We will certainly do it again. I just can't tell you when right now. It will be soon. Real soon. You can count on that.

This is the beginning of a great love affair." He made a bad attempt to sing the words. "Hey, that sounds like a good title for a song!" Frank laughed, "Go get some sleep. I'll see ya' soon, son."

The old priest pulled away, leaving Chui to his empty room. He went in and set his sax case on the little table. "God, I can't go to sleep yet. I am so wired. I am also hungry. I need to go out and get something to eat." He had decided the locked motel room was secure enough to leave his saxophone with its treasure. "If Customs can't find that money, no one can." He chuckled at his humor. He turned on the light and punched the "On" button of the remote. The TV screen was selling a fitness device. "That TV ought to make it seem like I am in here -- should be a good burglar alarm. I won't be gone long."

He began to walk along the Interstate 10 frontage road. He was tired of Denny's. There were some bright lights a block or two ahead. It was cool tonight, but his new sport coat was warm enough. The bright lights came closer. It was the Capri Restaurant and Lounge. The sign proclaimed that it was open. "That looks good to me." He walked in the door and entered the smoke-filled restaurant. There were pool tables with guys who looked like wannabe cowboys with big hats playing pool. A young girl with a very short skirt approached him. "You still serving food?" he asked.

"Sure, have a seat. Just sit wherever you want."

As his eyes became accustomed to the dim lights, Chui looked around and picked a table in the corner, away from the guys with the tall sombreros and the custom pool cue sticks. He sat down and plucked the menu from the rack on the table. "A hamburger and French fries sure sounds good."

"Can I get ya'all somethin' to drink?"

Chui hesitated. *"Don't I deserve a little treat tonight?"* He asked himself. *"Just one before I eat my burger. I can handle that. Just one won't matter, will it?"* He had convinced himself that he could handle just one drink. *"Just one and that's all."* He had plenty of money in his pocket. His own money he had worked for and earned tonight. These thoughts flashed by in a split second as he turned to the waitress and said, "Yeah, bring me a Vodka, on the rocks."

Chapter 27

The big charter bus had arrived well ahead of time. The driver had taken it to one of the two motels and had spent his time on the island lounging around, reading magazines. He was anxious to get going and finish his tour of duty for the charter bus company. The engine was running and the door was open as the group filed into the bus, sleepy eyed and yawning. It was just before 6 a.m. The sun was just peeping over the Gulf.

There had been no going away party last night. Most of the students were so tired they went right to sleep. Susie had slept alone in the cabana. Father Francisco had chosen to sleep in one of the empty bunks with two of the boys. He left all the supplies in the cabin with Susie and she had gotten up very early and packed everything, ready for the return trip.

Everything was loaded; the door was closed as the big bus rattled along the road over the causeway and back toward Del Rio. Cali and Johnny sat together on the return trip. Father Francisco was in his usual front seat with the supplies. Susie sat across from him, next to the window, all alone. She had not slept much last night and the rhythm of the big bus lulled her to sleep with her head bumping against the window. She had strange dreams about Jim and Cali and priests and wine and Nat King Cole.

The trip usually took seven or eight hours and by the time they had stopped in Laredo for a quick lunch, it added another half hour. It was about two in the afternoon when they pulled up to the school. Johnny's sister had come to pick him up and offered to take Cali and Susie home. They accepted. Jim was busy, playing at Jack's. By the time the mother and daughter got home, they were ready for a long nap. Susie saw the note left for her on the pillow. It said, *"I have wonderful news. I want to keep it a surprise. Hope you and Cali had a good time. I should be home about 4. I love you. Jim."* It was 3:30. He would be home shortly. She should be happy about that, but she dreaded seeing him. She felt very guilty about something and didn't even know what it was.

Chapter 28

A popular song spoke of "Fire and Rain." Both are essential to our well-being, but either one can lead to disaster, when left unchecked and without moderation. A drink or two is sometimes a good way to relax after a stressful and exciting night. Chui was on his fourth vodka. He had a hamburger sitting in front of him, with a pile of greasy French fries. They had hardly been touched. He was getting his eyes focused on the guys with the big hats and the Lone Star beer sign above the window. He finished the fourth and signaled the waitress over for another. "Ya might as well make it a derble – Uh, I mean a – you know -- put two shots in 'ere this time." He laughed at his unfunny joke and so did the girl in the short skirt.

"Comin' rat up. Somethin' wrong with the burger?"

"Oooh, nooo." Chui apologized. "I jush hadn't got to it yet. He picked up the big sandwich and opened his mouth and took a big bite. "Ish good." He spoke with his mouth full, dribbling catsup and juice out onto his sport coat and the table.

Chui's mind began to drift, as he sipped his fifth and sixth vodka on the rocks. He thought about tonight and how well he had played with three total strangers. His mind drifted back to his grandfather. His grandpa had taught him to improvise. They would sit in the yard and play together when he was only ten or so. Chui was a natural musician. He had musical talent that others did not have. He started with the clarinet and then the saxophone in the grade school band. Then he went into the junior high school band. His band director chastised him for improvising instead of playing the music as it was written. He laughed at himself at that memory. He must have been a real pain in the ass to that bandleader. But he played the clarinet and had "first chair" when he was a senior. He learned to play all the reed instruments. But his favorite was the tenor sax.

Grandpa Jim would get out his trumpet and he would play without music as they sat outside in the yard. One Sunday afternoon his grandfather said, "Let's play 'Whispering'." Grandpa played the song and Chui followed along in unison. Then, on that special, glorious Sunday, his grandfather told him, "You play the melody and just let me play something else." His grandfather played a wonderful contrapuntal melody. They were playing the same song but with different notes. "Grandpa, you gotta show me how to do that," he remembers saying. "OK, I'll play the melody and you try the other part." He remembers that first time he learned what it was like to improvise on the chords of a song. He never forgot that afternoon and especially right now, he was remembering so vividly, as he was letting the booze numb his brain again.

"Goddamn, that was great! My grandpa, Jim, taught me everything I know. Bless his heart" Chui was reaching way back into his memory. He began to recall a few things he didn't want to think about.

He didn't remember exactly how far back his memory went. But it was probably when he was about three or four years old. He groped for the recollection of arguments between his mother and his father. They lived in a little house on a big ranch. His Grandfather Vasquez had built it for them. It was a nice house, but he spent a lot of time in the big ranch house. That is where Abuelo Paco and Abuela Randa lived. They were his father's parents. He stayed there while his mom frequently went somewhere in town and his dad worked on the ranch. This day, his dad talked about joining the Air Force. He loved to watch the jet planes fly over the ranch. He wanted to learn to fly.

It hurt him to hear his parents arguing. They did it a lot. It was often about something he did not understand back then. He had come to understand, as he grew older and more mature, that it was about sex. He didn't quite know what, but there always seemed to be a problem. But this day it was about his father going away for a while to learn to fly airplanes. He remembered that he was very sad. He loved his dad very much. He was always good and kind to him. His mom was good but sometimes not so kind. She seemed to be angry a lot.

Chui was still trying to remember what was going on fifty years ago. He often thought about it, but somehow the booze made it more vivid in his mind just now. He sipped his vodka and ate a couple of French fries and tried to focus on the Lone Star beer sign. He was seeing two neon signs and knew there was only one. He closed one eye. Then he saw just one. *"That's pretty damn clever,"* he giggled to himself as he continued to wink each eye.

The pool sharks with the big cowboy hats glanced at him now and then. They laughed and shook their heads. The waitress in the short skirt kept an eye on him as he began to bob his head around as though it didn't want to behave. His thoughts began to get more and more bizarre and confused with each sip of the undiluted 80 proof vodka he rolled over his lips and into his stomach.

His dad did go away and join the Air Force. He went to OCS and was accepted into pilot training. Chui remembered the day he came home with his blue uniform and his little wings on his chest. He was so happy to see him. His mom was happy, too. Even Grandma and Grandpa Williams came over to the ranch. They didn't do that very often. And his dad stood up and made the big announcement. Chui remembered it well. He told everyone he had been accepted in the jet-training program. He shouted out loud! "I will be coming back to Del Rio and training in the T-33's! I will be right here at home for a while! Watch out, Papa, or I will chase you out of that back pasture and scare those sheep away." He explained that he couldn't come to the house for a few weeks, but maybe he could get away for a few hours on the weekends now and then. He would be just like any other cadet. Then Grandpa Jim slapped him on the back and told him not to get too cocky, he would be watching as the band marched down to the flight line every day. They joked about that. He remembered his dad saying to his Grandpa Jim, "Watch out, Mister Williams, I will become a second lieutenant and I will outrank you!" Then Grandpa Jim saluted him smartly and he saluted back. Then they hugged. Abuelo Paco said, "Well, I don't have to salute neither of you – If it wasn't for me paying my taxes, you wouldn't have no pay at all!" They all laughed. Chui was recalling what a nice day that was. His mother was there but didn't have much to say.

Chui stared at the beer sign again and it was blurry. He had to wipe his eyes with the paper napkin. He ordered another double vodka on the rocks.

Chapter 29

"Susanna." That is the pet name Jim used for his wife. "Where are you?"

"I'm in the bathroom, just a minute." Susie had taken time for a quick shower. She needed to wash away the sand but she also needed to make some decisions about what to tell Jim about this weekend. She had made her decision. She would tell him that she had too much to drink and got out of line with Father Francisco on the beach but nothing serious happened. She would tell him that there was a problem of some sort with Cali. She was acting even more strange than normal. She would take whatever punishment he might deem appropriate. It would not be right to live with this guilt. She was not sure what went on after she passed out, so she might just leave that part out. She was ready with her confession.

"Susie, look in the closet." Jim rushed into their bedroom.

"What a strange request," she thought, standing there in her robe. "What am I supposed to look for in the closet?" She opened the door and peered in at his uniforms all lined up.

"What do you see different? Look at the sleeves."

"There aren't any stripes. Did you get busted?"

"No, silly girl. Now look at the collars."

Susie pulled back the uniform shirt and looked at the collar. "What are these? They are bars with stripes on them. What do these mean?"

"I know you haven't seen this rank before. You are looking at an Air Force Officer. Look at my hat. See the big eagle on it? That means I am no longer an enlisted man – I was promoted by the Base Commander, Colonel Bainbridge. I am now a Warrant Officer. I will be called, 'Mr. Williams.' I am now the new Band Director for Laughlin Air Force Base."

Susie let out a yell that woke Cali up from her nap in her bedroom. She ran toward her husband, jumped and wrapped her bare legs around his waist and nearly knocked him over. Cali came out of her room and asked what was going on. "Cali, Daddy is an officer now. He got promoted while we were gone. He is going to be the new band director for the base."

"Oh yes, one more thing." Jim cupped his hand to his mouth as though he was saying something confidential. "We can move to Officer's housing and get one of those regular houses over there on the other side of the base. Cali ran over and put her arms around both of her parents. They all three jumped up and down as they shouted for joy. Susie thought her confession should probably be postponed until later. It was postponed forever.

Chapter 30

"Where the hell am I?" Chui Vasquez was squinting his eyes, trying to focus on the two faces looking down at him. He saw Punj come into focus. He had on his white turban. Then there was Father Frank. He had on his priest suit.

"You are in your room. You passed out at the Capri restaurant and went to sleep in your hamburger and fries." Frank was laughing so hard he could hardly talk.

"What's so God damned funny, you frigging priest. You are supposed to be kind and helpful." Chui had not quite sobered up.

Frank finally got his breath. "You should have seen yourself with a vodka in one hand and a French fry in the other, passed out with your face in your plate. You had lettuce up your nose! And all the cowboys were looking at you, shaking their heads. Didn't I tell you to stay off that shit?" Frank laughed harder, showing no sympathy.

"You sure as hell don't sound very priest like."

"You are going to think 'priest like' when I get through with you. We are going to have a talk, ole buddy. I am going to tell you a story."

"Well, first, how did I get here. Last I remember, I was remembering stuff and squinting at a beer sign and trying to get it to focus. Did I pay my bill?"

"Yes, I paid it for you," Punj finally spoke up. "They found your room key in your coat pocket and called to see if anyone knew you. I called your priest friend here and he said to meet him at the Capri. They said you had passed out in your hamburger and had lettuce up your nose." He chuckled at the thought. "We got you in the car and brought you back here." Punj was laughing hilariously.

"Damn, you guys don't take anything serious, do you?"

"I know your Hindu friend here isn't supposed to drink, but I have had a drink or two in my day. That is why I need to tell you a story."

"I'll leave you two to your tales of the frailties of the demon rum." Punj left and went back to his apartment. It was 3 a.m.

"Do you remember when you went to Mass?" Father Frank began his tale. "You recall that the priest served you a little sip of wine? Well, the priest had a sip himself. And he did that several times a day. And some of us got to like that stuff really well, and we had a slug or two or five or nine when we got back home." Frank stood up and began to pace around the motel room as he talked. "Some of us went out and bought some hard stuff, just to get that nice buzz faster. And some of us got to where we couldn't live without that hard stuff. It was easy to mumble the words. They are all in Latin. So it was easy to keep this problem hidden from everyone. The church didn't seem to mind, as long as I did my duties." Frank paused and gathered his thoughts. "But only for a while. When a priest began to fall down during Mass, or forgot to show up for a wedding or a christening -- then it was time to do something about it. I was one of those priests, Chui. I have been there. I know what you are going through. That is why I am here. I want to help you." He pulled up a chair and sat down across from Chui. He looked him in the eye, as he got serious. "I am an alcoholic. I am a drunk! I was removed from my church and sent off to a private little home in the Jemez Mountains, near Santa Fe, New Mexico. We made things, trinkets and souvenirs. Some of us did artwork. The place was passed off as a monastery for monks. *We* were the Monks. But the fact is, we were all drunks. Drunken priests who needed to dry out."

The priest stopped for a minute, got up and put his hands behind his back and looked at the wall. "As the years went on, we were allowed to leave for short periods of time. It was a Wednesday afternoon. I remember it so well, even today. I went to Santa Fe and walked into the La Fonda Hotel. They had a piano there, so I asked if I could play a few tunes. They told me it would be fine, so I did. It was in the bar, and I decided if I could play in a bar and stay off the hooch, I could make it. I found an AA group. I joined the 12-step program. I began to help other drunks. I hid the fact that I was a priest for a long time. I was just 'Frank the piano man'."

Chui was wide eyed and totally engrossed in Frank's story. He was sobering up fast. "What happened after that?"

"I was there for several years, living in that monastery and playing in the bar in Santa Fe. Eventually, I decided I could do more good as a priest than just a piano player in a bar. So I showed up one day in my priest suit. My regulars were transfixed when I sat down to play that evening. I told them I was a priest but I was also an alcoholic and I couldn't deny either fact any longer. You know what they did?"

"What happened? What did they do?"

"They cheered, Chui, they clapped and cheered. They came up to me and shook my hand and hugged me."

Frank wiped away a tear running down his cheek as he recalled the moment. "I went back to the monastery and called the bishop and asked to be reinstated as a priest. I told them I was cured. Guess what happened?" Frank did not wait for a response. "The Archbishop of Santa Fe denied my request. He said I was not suited for this work. He said someone would find out about my past and the church would suffer for it."

"Well, how did you get back your authority?"

"Well, I heard about a bishop in El Paso, who maybe was a drunk himself in his day. I didn't know for sure. But, I called him. He told me to come down and talk. I left the monastery and drove down here. He said he would take a chance on me. He gave me back my life. I'll remember him forever for that." Frank teared up again then regained his composure. "And here I am. I've been here ever since."

The old priest suddenly had a total change in posture. "Chui." He was very serious now. "You are a drunk! Now, are you going to get off your ass and make something of yourself, or am I going to need to kick your ass again. Let me assure you, I will kick your ass as many times as it takes. You cannot drink *just one* drink like the rest of mankind. You must drink *zero* drinks for the rest of your life and I will be there to see that you do that. If you fall off the wagon, I will put you back on, just as other guys did me. I have elected myself to be your guardian, as long as I live. But let me assure you, I am NOT your guardian a*ngel*."

There was what musicians call a "Grand Pause" in the room. Neither man said anything for several minutes. Then Chui broke the silence, "Father Frank, did you ever have a church in Del

Rio, Texas?" The priest grew very quiet. He was waiting for that question. "I remember a priest back when I was a kid, who left the parish suddenly and disappeared. I was pretty young, but it was quite a scandal in the church. They talked about it for years afterwards. I couldn't help but notice the name on your passport. Were you called Father Francisco back in Del Rio?"

Chapter 31

One of Jim's first chores was to go over to the mess hall. He was not there to eat. He was there to find a musician. "I need to see Sgt. Seagrove," he told an airman third class who was stirring a big cauldron of something.

"Yes, sir." The airman saluted Jim. It was his first salute as a new officer.

"Tell him, Sarg – uh, that is, *Mister* Williams is here. *I have got to get used to this.*

Bob Seagrove was a rather heavyset man with a round smiling face. He sweated a lot and today was no exception. He came through the swinging door and stopped in his tracks. "Well, Goddamn. Where the hell did your stripes go? And what the hell is that brass on your collar? You can get court marshaled for impersonating an officer, you know." He grabbed Jim by the hand and signaled him to a table to sit down. "Bring MISTER Williams and me some coffee," he commanded the young airman.

"Bob, as you can see, the Colonel has made me a Warrant Officer and given me the authority to organize a band – a REAL band. We will all have AFPC's as bandsmen. You will never cook again! You are the first one I have contacted. I am assuming you will go with me.

"I don't have to re-up, do I?"

"That is up to you. But, no, you don't have to re-up to be transferred to the band. What do you say? I can have you out of here this week. I need an assistant and you would be perfect."

"Is the Pope a Catholic? Does a bear shit in the woods? Is there a better way to put it than 'Hell Yes'?" He shouted so loud the kitchen crew came to the door to see what was going on.

"I thought you might find that acceptable. I'll put you down."

Jim went to the personnel office next and met with Chuck Berghetti. He got the same response. He now had two. He contacted Bernie Schmidt and he agreed, after he checked with his wife.

The next few days brought some response to an ad in the base paper and some posters he had put around the base. He had nearly fifty responses to his request for musicians. Most of them were not qualified, but five men showed some promise.

The city of Del Rio had built a new airport. The old airport was on government property, right across the highway from the base. The Del Rio weather bureau office occupied one end of the old airport terminal. The rest of the building was vacant. So, since it belonged to the US government, the base had taken it over. This was a perfect location for the new band. It housed Jim's new office and a big open room, which would become the rehearsal hall.

The colonel had made good his promise to contact the other bases in Texas and recruit some musicians. There were five men soon to be transferred to Del Rio. So far he had twelve bandsmen. This was the beginning of the 510th Air Force Band of Laughlin Air Force Base, Texas, under the command of Warrant Officer James Williams.

Chapter 32

It is May, 1950. Commencement was two days ago. Both Cali and Johnny graduated at the top of their class. Both were members of the National Honor Society. They had several offers from universities. Neither had decided where to go to college.

Father Francisco was sitting in his office. The bell rang, signaling that someone needed to have confession heard. The bell had been connected to the door of the booth. Neither priest wanted to miss anyone who needed help. Father Francisco pushed his chair back from the desk and walked toward the door to his side of the booth. He wished he hadn't been interrupted, and felt rather ashamed of his thought. But, it was part of his duty as a priest. Confession was very important in the life of a true Catholic. It was early afternoon, not a usual time for confession.

He had not seen the young girl enter the church and rush to the booth. She sat down and closed the door behind her.

"May I hear your sins? May I offer you a chance to confess and be forgiven?" Father spoke the words to the screen window that separated him from the person in the other side of the booth.

"May I help you?" The priest spoke again to the screen.

"Father -- Father Francisco!" She whispered the words through the screen. "It's Caliente -- Cali. I need to talk to you."

"Cali, You are not supposed to tell me who you are," the priest whispered back. "You are supposed to be anonymous. And you are not supposed to know who I am."

"I don't know the rules. I am not a Catholic. I just need to talk to you."

"Cali, you can talk to me right here. I can hear your confessions and we will decide what to do. I'll just tell you what to do to be forgiven. That's all there is to it."

"No. No. You don't understand. It's more important than that. I MUST talk to you face to face but I don't know where your office is. I thought if I came in this little room....."

"Cali, I can't. I'm not even supposed to be doing this. It's not the way it's done."

"I don't *care* how it's done, Father." Cali was getting impatient with this ritual she didn't understand. "I've GOT to talk to you."

"OK. OK. OK. Calm down. What's the problem?"

"Well, it's a little personal," Cali stammered and finally explained. "You see, girls my age have a period every month."

"Yes, Cali, I do know something about the female anatomy. I do hope you aren't about to tell me….."

Cali cut him off. The words erupted from her mouth. "I have not had any periods for two months, and I have a stomachache every morning. I crave stuff, weird stuff. Father," her voice was silent for a few seconds and so was his. Then she spilled out the words the priest was afraid she was going to say. "I think I am pregnant."

Dead silence. Neither spoke for several seconds. Cali spoke first. "Father? Are you there? Are you still there?"

"Cali. Come out of the booth and turn left. There is a big door ahead of you. That is my office. I will see you there shortly. We need to talk immediately."

Father Francisco was seated behind his desk when she entered. He had poured a glass of clear liquid and was sipping on it

"Father, I need to get rid of this baby. I need to get an abortion."

"Oh, God, no, Cali. You can't do that. It's against the law. And besides, it's totally against everything we believe in here."

"But, I have to do something." She was beginning to sob.

Father Francisco took another sip from his glass and asked her a one-word question. "Johnny?"

"I haven't told him yet."

"Do you think he -- will he be responsible?"

"I think so, Father, I think so. He is such a good person. I know he will be responsible."

"The first thing you need to do is tell Johnny. And the very next thing you need to do is tell your parents. That is going to be hard. But the sooner, the better. And the third thing you need to do is get Johnny and come and see me. We will get your marriage consummated just as soon as possible.

Cali left the church wondering if she still might be able to get an abortion. In 1950, abortion was not legal, but there were places that would do it for a price. This was what she was thinking she would propose to her parents when she called her mother and said she needed to talk to her and her dad as soon as possible.

Susie called Jim and told him that Cali needed to talk to them. She said it sounded important. Cali had been busy and rather distant for the past several weeks. But she chalked it up to her busy senior year. It was a nice change for her to want to talk to them. Jim said he was not doing anything that couldn't be done later and he would be right home. He rolled out of the parking lot of his new quarters, across the highway and through the base gate. The AP saluted him smartly as he waved him past. *"That is pretty nice,"* he thought. *"I think I like this officer stuff."*

Cali had opened a coke and was eating some cottage cheese. "What in the world are you eating," her mother asked.

"Oh, I thought I might like some cottage cheese with this coke. I have been eating some weird stuff lately."

"Well, here comes your dad."

Jim took off his hat, opened the refrigerator door and pulled out a cold beer. "OK, what's up? You decided where you are going to college? We probably can't afford it, but we'll see what we can do." He uncapped the beer and took a sip.

"I need you to sit down a minute. I have something important to tell you." They both suddenly became concerned at the serious tone of her voice. She had their attention. She sat her coke and cheese down on the table. "Mom. Dad. I

146

am going to tell you something you are not going to want to hear. I need to ask you a question. How would you feel about being grandparents?"

Chapter 33

It is said by a very wise man, "Sex, politics and religion is the dreaded triumvirate to avoid in any discussion." If you have all three, the problem is about as bad as it gets. And so it was with the first meeting on the subject of their respective offspring. It was held at the big ranch house in the formal dining room around a gigantic, solid oak, antique table. Paco and Aranda, headed the steadfast Catholic, Hispanic family. They had a daughter in San Antonio studying at the convent. Anna Maria would become a nun if things went as planned. Speaking for the other team were Jim and Susie Williams. They had rarely attended a church of any sort, except, maybe for Christmas or Easter at the base chapel.

Niceties were exchanged, drinks offered and some small talk was had. Then, time for some serious discussion on the matter of their children.

The notion of an abortion was brought up briefly. The Vasquez side of the debate indicated in no uncertain terms that abortion was non-negotiable. Not only was it illegal, it was a cardinal sin. The Pope had so decreed and so it was. No debate. The Williams team could see that it was a dead issue and gave up quickly.

Next was the matter of marriage. Each team politely, but in no uncertain terms, accused the other team's offspring of causing the pregnancy. Each politely suggested that their offspring was not easily drawn into such a copulation event without a great deal of seduction and a measure of loose morals from the other partner. They eventually agreed that it was, perhaps, a fifty-fifty deal. They also, justifiably, agreed that there was nothing to be gained by arguing that point. The deed had been committed and the results must be dealt with.

Cali and Johnny were present, seated on the living room couch during these discussions, and not allowed to speak. They were, after all, the culprits, the criminals, and had no say in the matter. They were reminded that, although they were barely eighteen, they were too immature and not yet able to make these important decisions for themselves. They sat, quietly, and listened to their lives being charted by their parents.

The final decision was a compromise. Cali would go to a good Catholic home for unwed mothers. There was one in Uvalde, about 80 miles from Del Rio. It was operated by a group of nice, matronly Sisters. They had wonderful connections with the outside world. They would see to it that Cali was taken out of society before she put on any more weight and embarrassed her parents. The four had agreed that no mention would be made of Johnny's involvement. For this compromise, the Valdez's would agree to pay for the care at the home for the next seven months or so. When the not-so-blessed event took place, the half-Mexican, half-Anglo baby would be put up for adoption.

Cali could then get on with her life and so could Johnny. The matter was settled.

And so it was this decision that prompted Cali to rush to the church. This time she did not enter the confession booth. She ran right through the door to Father Francisco's office and burst into tears. He grabbed her and they hugged each other as she shook and cried. She sobbed out the words, "adoption," and Uvalde. He finally managed to get her calmed down and heard the decision that had been made by the parents. He took a deep breath and tried to clear his mind and be neutral and rational. "I am sure it is the best thing," he lied to her. "I am sure you will be much better off in the future. You have college to think about; Johnny has college, too. You both are so bright and capable. You must think of your future." He hugged her for a long time and she continued to sob on his shoulder. He grabbed his handkerchief from his pocket and dried her eyes. He kissed her cheek, longer than he should have. He tightened his grip on her body, much tighter than he should have. He pulled her closer and closer. He reluctantly let her go and poured himself a drink. She felt better, but not good. She had some thinking to do about this.

Chapter 34

Uvalde, Texas, is about halfway between Del Rio and San Antonio. It is the home of Dale Evans, the famous wife of the famous cowboy star, Roy Rogers. The signs and plaques around the little town readily advertise this fact. It is also the home of the Sisters of Mercy home for wayward women. This is NOT readily advertised around town. It is, as a matter of fact, kept a secret. There is no evidence of the big house's purpose for existing. It is austere and enormous. A circle drive brings visitors or customers right to the small portico and the front door. The grounds are pretty. There is green grass and there are lots of trees. A high red wooden fence encloses a huge back yard where clotheslines sport all sorts of white sheets and pillowcases blowing in the wind. If one could see over the fence, one would see young girls, in varying degrees of pregnancy, hanging up the clothes or just sitting around in their plain maternity dresses. Some are laughing but most are not. Cali sits alone. Her long blond hair is now in a bun. She has gained several pounds and her tummy has begun to protrude. She has been there for over a month. She has been fed well, but along with the food has come a good measure of guilt-ridden platitudes. She has been made to feel guilty for her "sin." It was called the "original sin," she was told. She has been injected with the teachings of the church each day, sometimes several times. She has been required to attend mass every day and to pretend she is a

Catholic. She has gone along with this ritual, not because she wants to, but because she agreed. But mostly she has gone along with it because Father Francisco said it was the right thing to do.

However, Cali was never one to do things she did not wish to do. She has kept to herself and away from the other girls. Most of them are Mexican and speak Spanish to each other. Although she learned Spanish in high school, this is a brand of the language called "Tex-Mex," and is often not understandable by non-Hispanics. She is sitting in a lounge chair under a big Mesquite tree in the back yard. Her legs are straight and she is trying to get comfortable with the extra weight her abdomen has recently acquired. She has been sitting and thinking since morning mass and breakfast. A slight smile can be detected on her lips. It might be mistaken for a smirk. She has made a decision.

She struggles to get herself up from the lounge chair and waddles to the back door. She proceeds to the "front desk" to use the phone. The sister who is normally seated there guarding the entrance has gone to the bathroom. Cali seizes the opportunity and grabs the phone and makes a collect call to the Iturria Ranch. Aranda answers in her soft voice. She whispers into the phone, "Momma Randa, this is Cali. I need to speak to Johnny. Is he there?"

"Cali, you aren't supposed to call anyone."

"Please, Randa, Mrs. Vasquez, it is important. Please, I just need to talk to him for a minute, that's all, just one minute."

Aranda Vasquez has been very subservient through all this business. She has not really had a say in the matter. She was expected to do as she was told in the decision making process. It mattered not what she thought – it mattered only what Paco thought. That was the Mexican way. El Esposo is El Jefe. She heard a plea in Cali's voice that only a woman could detect. She decided it was her turn to exert some authority. "Just a minute, Corazon. I will get him."

What seemed like an hour was only a few seconds. "Cali. Is everything OK?" Finally he was there. Johnny's voice sounded like an angel.

"No, it's not OK, Johnny. I have to get out of here!" Cali was speaking in a loud whisper, cupping the phone in her hands. "You've got to come and get me. We can handle this thing by ourselves. I love you. I'll have our baby but I want it my way – our way."

The hesitation gave Cali some trepidation. Finally, Johnny's voice firmly answered her. "I'll be over there as soon as I can get there. I love you, too. I am so glad you called. I have been thinking about this. Yes, yes. We'll work it out ourselves. It will take me an hour or so but I'll leave right now." The sister had just returned from the bathroom and began chastising Cali.

"You aren't supposed to use the phone without permission, young lady. Who were you calling?"

"Well, you weren't here. I just wanted to talk to my mom for a minute, but no one answered." Cali now had a big smile on her face for the first time since she had checked in to the Sisters of Mercy home for unwed mothers. She went to her room, shut her door and wrapped all her meager belongings in a bed sheet. She could see the circle drive from her upstairs window. It seemed like an eternity, but finally the familiar blue pickup truck with "Iturria Ranch" painted on its door pulled into the drive. She grabbed the sheet, threw it over her shoulder like a hobo and flew down the stairs and past the front desk. "You can't leave here without permission!" The sister in her black habit and white collar shouted as Cali ran past her.

"You watch me!"

Johnny had gotten out of the truck. "Get in. Let's go before they grab me. She threw her belongings in the bed of the truck, leaped into the passenger's side and slammed the door just as Johnny jumped in behind the steering wheel. The rear wheels spun in the gravel driveway as the blue truck sped out and onto the highway. A few miles onto Highway 90 toward Del Rio, there was a small picnic area. Johnny pulled in, stopped the truck and turned toward Cali. Before he could say a

154

word, she grabbed him by his curly, black hair and pulled him to her. Tears streamed down her cheeks as she fell over backwards in the truck seat and gave him the longest and hardest kiss she had ever given anyone in her entire life.

Chapter 35

By the time they had passed under the worn-out sign and the big iron gate of the Iturria Ranch, it was late afternoon. The Sister at the home in Uvalde had already called the ranch and talked to Aranda. Paco was out feeding the sheep. She called Susie and told her that Johnny had left and she thought he was on his way to Uvalde. Susie called Jim and they came immediately to the ranch house. Paco was there by now. They waited for some word. They each expressed their dismay and concern about their children. "I don't care what they have done. I just want to know they are safe." Susie was the most vociferous. Paco paced around. Aranda smiled and brought more coffee. Jim and Paco tried to make small talk about local politics. None of them could concentrate on anything much except their children's welfare.

Aranda had stationed herself at the front window. She could see the front lane from there. She would be the first to see any activity. She was thinking how much she was opposed to this arrangement in the first place. She would much prefer to have them get married and have their child and keep it. She was thinking what a wonderful thing it might be to have a grandchild, a baby to hold and care for. But she had been denied any real vote in the matter. Paco had spoken for both of them, as he always did.

It had been about five hours since Johnny's sudden exodus. All four parents were having second thoughts about their decision in this matter. They were quietly wishing they might have talked it over with their kids and been a little less hasty before forcing this decision onto them.

"Here they come! Here they come!" It was Aranda who spotted the blue truck first. "Gracias, Dio. Thank God, they are safe." She crossed herself, unconsciously.

The four parents spilled out of the ranch house en mass. Expressions of anger and relief were spouting from their mouths as they ran toward the two renegades. Each parent both hugged and reprimanded his respective offspring as the group moved toward the ranch house.

"We need to talk to you." It was Cali who spoke first.

"Where have you been?" Susie interrupted.

"Mom, please shut up and give us a chance to talk."

It was Johnny's turn. "We don't like your choices for us." He had never spoken in this manner to his, or anyone's, parents. He had authority in his voice. "We didn't even get a chance to express our opinion during all this mess. We are of legal age and we have a right to make our own decisions, and we are going to."

Paco rose and was about to speak. "Papa, sit down. Please be quiet and let me speak. We already tried it your way. I know you thought you were doing the best thing for me. But this is my problem, not yours. I need to work it out myself. Cali and I -- together." Paco, who was not used to being spoken to in that manner, had a startled look on his face but he sat down.

"You see," Cali spoke next, "Johnny and I have decided the best solution is for us to keep this baby. That can't be too bad, can it? You all will be grandparents. Is that so bad?" All four parents grew very still, mulling over the prospect of that eventuality. There was no response for several minutes. Everyone stared at the two eighteen-year-olds in front of them. Finally it was Aranda who jumped up and spoke. "You will need to be married soon. We will have a big wedding! We will have it here at the ranch."

"No, Mama," Juanito interrupted his mother. "We have just come from a visit with Father Francisco."

Cali spoke next. "We were married about an hour ago. We are now Mr. and Mrs. Juan Vasquez!" Cali produced a signed and stamped license with Father Francisco's signature on it. "Wouldn't all you future grandparents like to be the first to congratulate the newlyweds?"

Chapter 36

And so it was on December 25th, 1950, Christmas morning, around dawn, a child was born and he was called Jesus; Jesus William Vasquez. He was given that name for several reasons. It was Christmas. But more importantly, it was his father's middle name and his paternal grandfather's last name. Paco elected himself as chief of the naming process; but since the baby was half Mexican and half Anglo, Jim insisted that he represent both factions, and thus the middle name would be William. Neither Cali nor Johnny had much to say about the choice of names. They were just happy to have a healthy baby boy and loving parents and grandparents. And so, the birth certificate officially named the parents as Juan Jesus Vasquez and Caliente Susanne Williams Vasquez. The baby would very soon be given a pseudonym. Abuelo Paco came up with an old Spanish nickname for Jesus. And, thus, except for legal matters, for the rest of his life he would be called Chui, which, Paco explained, "En Engles, es como Chewy." On this Christmas morning in 1950, Chui Vasquez welcomed himself to the world.

Chapter 37

A house that had been reserved for the workers had been built at the rear of the big ranch house. It was normally filled with Mexican laborers. Often there were entire families living there, working on the big ranch along with Paco and his sons. Aranda suggested that they might fix that house up and remodel it and maybe the "kids" could live there for awhile. Cali and Johnny had moved back and forth between each parent's home before the baby came. But, now they needed a more permanent residence. Paco thought remodeling the "guest" house was a grand idea, and took credit for it. He set about to hire workers to remodel the "Mexican" house. He hoped to have it ready for them as soon as the baby came. He was right on schedule. They were able to move in when Cali came home from the hospital with little Jesus.

Even though Jim and Susie had moved into larger officer's quarters, their house was still rather small. It was quite small, compared to the ranch house. But, the Vasquez's had grown rather fond of the Williams's and visa versus. They had regular visitations. When Cali moved into her new residence, about 500 feet from the back door of the big house, her parents were free to visit any time. And they did so, frequently.

"Mister" Williams had his complete twenty-piece band now, and he was able to make music for whatever the occasion. He could play in parades and did so regularly. The small band frequently went to the small towns in west Texas to play for various events. His versatile band could also play for dances. He was called to play for formal events at the Officers Club. There was a graduation of cadets every month. There was the visitation of VIP's. There was even a visit from President Eisenhower. The band played the ruffles and flourishes and "Hail to the Chief." The president was there for only about ten minutes, but no matter, the band played "honors" for him. Jim still had his small group, the Dixiecats. They were all members of the band and played at various places around town. He maintained his "friendship" with the base commander, Col. Bainbridge. They could not be close friends, but they were compadres, of sorts.

And so, there seemed to be happiness abounding with Johnny and Cali Vasquez. But all was not as it seemed. Behind the walls of the little house, Cali was not happy. She visited Father Francisco regularly and discussed her problems with him in his office. He looked forward to these visits and took the opportunity to "relax" with a glass or so of his favorite clear liquid.

Cali was concerned about sex. It was a touchy subject to be discussing with a priest, but Father Francisco seemed to be comfortable with the subject. One would think she would be having a problem with Johnny's sexual demands on her. That is what Father Francisco usually heard as he counseled his parishioners. But Cali told the priest quite a different story. It was she whose sexual demands were not being met. "He seems to be in another world," she would say. "He is always tired and not interested. We haven't had sex for months. What's wrong with me?"

"There is nothing wrong with you, believe me. I am sure this new baby is a big strain on him both physically and mentally. He loves you. He will come around."

Cali went away with confidence that the priest was right. Perhaps she was just too demanding. She would just stay busy and things would get better.

Cali tried to stay busy. She had begun some correspondence courses from the University of Wisconsin correspondence school. One of her interests was biology. She buried herself in the books and faithfully sent the lessons back. She anxiously looked forward to the return envelope with her graded tests. She was making straight A's. After she finished the biology course, she started on a course in Latin. She already spoke Spanish rather well, and found the Latin was the root to both Spanish and English in a lot of ways. She was getting along great with the dead language. These courses were a Godsend. It got her mind off her problems. Time passed. Months turned into a couple of years. Little Jesus had long since learned to walk and talk. He was such a perfect baby. He was doted upon by everyone, but he handled it well. His Grandpa Vasquez took him in the truck to feed the sheep. He learned to ride a horse quite well. His Grandpa Williams took him to the band rehearsals and let him swing the baton and pretend to direct, as the musicians rehearsed. He was the band mascot. But his mother and father were not doing well. There were problems to be dealt with in the Juan Vasquez family.

Johnny's twin brothers had finished their basic training in California long ago. They were sent to Korea and saw some combat, but remained unscathed
Each earned a number of medals and sent pictures of themselves regularly. They looked brave and handsome. Everyone was so proud, especially Johnny. Neither Ramon nor Damon had married, and they had no children that they were aware of. They had been reassigned to the basic training base in California, and had been appointed as drill sergeants, to train new recruits. This would keep them safe from combat for several years.

Juanito was working on the ranch for his father. He and Cali had a good life. Their home was rent-free. They had plenty of food. Little Chui was well fed and well dressed. Each grandmother tried to outdo the other in providing things. Each grandfather tried to outdo the other in providing toys, cowboy boots and other little boy essentials. Cali had a ready-made baby-sitter anytime she needed it. Life appeared to be happy and contented. But, she and Father Francisco knew differently.

Chapter 38

"Why did my passport make you ask me if I had served in Del Rio? Father Frank was answering Chui's question as he sat in the chair next to Chui's bed in the Motel 6. It was nearly 4 in the morning.

"I didn't mean to pry, but I saw your name. It said Francisco Ortiz Y Jimenez." Chui had sobered up considerably since he had passed out in the Capri Lounge a few hours ago. His mind was much clearer than it had been just an hour ago. "And I have a few other questions while I am at it."

"Such as?"

"Why were you standing on the corner yesterday, listening to me play? How did you know I was at this motel? Why did you say you know more than I think you know? How's that for a start?"

The priest sprouted a sly grin. "You are a pretty damn inquisitive drunk tonight, aren't you? Well, Mr. Vasquez, what would you think if I told you I handed you that passport on purpose? What would you say if I told you I was waiting for that question?" Frank stood up and stretched and yawned. "I told you when you woke up I had a story to tell you. I only told you part of it. But I am too tired right now. It is nearly four in the morning. I need to go home and get some rest and you need to get some sleep. It is Sunday morning and I have duties to perform."

"C'mon, preacherman, you can't just leave me hanging off the cliff."

"Sure I can. But I will tell you this much. Yes, years ago I did serve in Del Rio. I have known you since you were born, Son. I baptized you. I performed the marriage ceremony for your parents. I know you have not had a perfect life. I know your dad disappeared and no one knew what happened to him. I know your mother left you when you were young. I know your grandparents raised you. And, I also know I will call you tomorrow after my church duties and we will have a long talk."

With that the priest left room 108 and as he closed the door he turned and said one more time. "You get some rest and I will see you later."

Chui was in no mood to get any rest. "I sure would like a drink," he thought. Then he corrected himself. "I sure would like a cup of coffee." He got up and went to the bathroom. He looked at himself in the mirror. His face was a mess and so was his hair. He cleaned himself up and combed his hair. He grabbed his key card from the dresser, went out the door and headed for Denny's all night restaurant. He ordered a double coffee to go and returned to his room. "I *gotta* think. I gotta try and remember a few things about my life." He sat down in the chair where the priest had been sitting, took a few sips of his coffee and began to think. He closed his eyes and forced himself to remember.

Somehow, his life began to take a wrong turn when his dad joined the Air Force and became a jet pilot.

Chapter 39

Chui struggled to go back in his memory. It would require about fifty years of regression. It was 1955. He recalled in vivid detail when his dad had announced to his mother that he was going to join the Air Force and apply for flight training. His mother cried about it, but he was led to believe it was tears of joy. It was, in fact, tears of sadness. The fact is, the little family had not been successful. They were forced to become responsible adults far earlier than they should have. They never got the opportunity to be "just kids." They had never had that opportunity to sing *"those were the days my friend, we thought they'd never end."*

This move was an attempt to save the marriage by forcing a separation without admitting they needed it. A divorce was out of the question, especially since they had been married in the church. They genuinely tried hard to make a success of their lives, in spite of their youth. They had all the support anyone could ask for by all four of their parents. Cali was getting quite a few hours of college credit accumulated. She was not sure just what she would do with these credits, but she was excited about her eagerness to learn. Johnny was working on the ranch with his father and being paid quite well for his labor. But he was often caught day dreaming, as those jet planes flew overhead on their way back to the base in the afternoon. He saw himself as a pilot behind the

167

stick of one of those planes. His two brothers were now well along in their careers in the Marines. The Korean War was practically over. He reached his decision as he looked up and saw one of the T-33's overhead so close he could reach up and touch it. He turned his brown horse around and headed back home, knowing what he must do.

It was a sad day when he left but everyone was proud when he was accepted for flight training. They were even more excited when a few months later he was accepted for T-33 jet training right in his back yard, literally.

Chui did not know all the details of this pivotal point in his life. But he knew it was significant. His coffee had cooled, and he took a big drink and closed his eyes again.

His dad had not only become a jet pilot, he had gone off to someplace or other to learn to fly the newest and latest jet planes. He had become quite an expert. His family didn't really know what his training was all about. It was "classified." He was able to come home occasionally. It was always a joyous event. Jim and Susie would come to the ranch and they all would have a party and celebrate Johnny's success and hear some "war stories." Cali smiled her forced smile and pretended to be a happy wife and mother. Chui remembered that part quite well. He remembered that his father had been a pilot for about two years when he announced that he had been assigned, for the second time, to Laughlin Air

Force Base. He would be a flight instructor. He could live at home if he wanted. That made everyone very happy, especially Chui. He was about eight, he recalled as he shifted his weight in the chair in the motel room and finished off his cold coffee.

His mind wandered back, again. By this time he was a budding musician. He loved to play the clarinet in the junior band. His Grandpa Jim had helped him learn. He practiced a lot. He remembered progressing into the high school band. He learned the saxophone. Jim had encouraged him to learn and gave him an old tenor sax, which was going to be discarded by the Air Force Band. He loved that old saxophone. He shined it all up. It had such a mellow tone and he took to it immediately.

He fast-forwarded his thoughts. His high school grades were not spectacular, but certainly acceptable, but his music abilities were very special. He had played frequently with his grandfather's little combo. Grandpa Jim always "showcased" him. That made him feel great, making him perform all the better. He was a whiz at improvising. He could sight-read music like a champ. He had applied to several universities, one of which was North Texas. This school was known for its music program. Chui smiled at himself and even chuckled out loud, as he thought about the day he got the letter. He had been accepted at North Texas. "This is better than Julliard!" He had quipped to his grandfather. Jim had chided him about it not being as good as the Jordan Music Conservatory, but plenty good enough. Jordon was Grandpa's alma mater. He was only joking. Jim was a very proud grandfather. He volunteered to drive him all the way up to Dallas and then to Denton and the university campus. His grandfather was a little teary-eyed when he left North Texas University that day. Chui had been given a brand new Selmer tenor sax as a graduation gift. All four grandparents had chipped in. Jim had suggested it. Chui opened his eyes and looked across the motel room. There was his sax case on the table. After all these years, he still had it.

His recollections were beginning to get clearer now. He wanted to remember his mother when he was small. She was a good mother, he thought, but rather preoccupied. It was like she had her mind on something else all the time. She would often ask him to repeat his question, telling him she didn't hear what he said. He often would tell her to forget it, it wasn't important. He wished he could remember better. He knew that she left him with his grandparents one day. But the memories were vague. It was probably just as well.

The fact is, he was eleven. She had taken him to her parents for a visit. She had brought a lot of clothes and things. She had been to see Father Francisco two days before. She had been told by the older priest, Aranda's brother, Father Cantu, that he had gone away for a while. She was

170

afraid something was up. Over the years when she had visited him for their "counseling" sessions, he had been gradually more unresponsive. He always had his drink handy and sipped on it. He almost fell asleep at his desk one day. Cali was no dummy. She knew what was in the glass. It was booze of some kind, probably gin or vodka. It made him rather funny and loose. But lately he had been difficult to understand. He would stray from the subject. She had heard that he had recently fallen down at the alter during a mass. He had tried a couple of times to get a little too intimate with her. She didn't deny that it was appealing, but not under these circumstances. She needed to fend him off and he apologized profusely and begged her forgiveness. He said he didn't know what came over him. The fact is, he was drunk. She knew he had been drinking a lot lately and was drunk nearly all the time. And so, when she heard that he was gone for a while, it was no surprise. But it was a sad time. He was her only salvation and a true friend. She could talk to him about *anything*, and he was nonjudgmental. Now he was gone.

Johnny was spending most of his time at the base. He had a room in the BOQ. He said he needed to be right there with his cadets. Cali had long since accepted the fact that he was not interested in much of an intimate relationship with her. She was not getting any younger. She needed to make some decisions. Some of these decisions were not going to be popular with her family.

Chapter 40

Chui struggled with memories of his mother. He switched his thoughts to his dad. He was such a wonderful dad, he was so kind and gentle and caring; but he was seldom home. He would come home on weekends but often stayed at the base all week. He remembered the day when the family was having one of their gatherings. It was probably Thanksgiving. Chui groped for the date but couldn't put his finger on it. His dad had put on his "civvies" and was chatting with everyone. Grandpa Jim was joking with him about getting outranked. Johnny had been promoted to Captain by now. Chui remembered hearing his father say something about a special assignment. Everyone got very quiet. He did not comprehend exactly what that meant but felt it was not good news. Everyone congratulated him, but it all seemed to be with some trepidation. The cold war was not so cold and special assignments could mean hazardous situations.

The fact is, Jim Williams had been called into the Base Commander's office a few weeks before. He was now Brigadier General Bainbridge. Jim had been to the General's office so many times since his first nerve-shattering visit, that it was no big deal. Jim had now been promoted to First Lieutenant. He bounced into the General's office with authority. "I have an appointment with the General."

The second lieutenant at the desk jumped up and said "Yes, sir, Lieutenant Williams. I will tell him you are here. "

"Boy, I remember the first time I was here," Jim thought to himself. *"Things sure have changed."*

"Jim. Come in and have a seat. How are things going with our band?" They shook hands. Jim was glad the general had a proprietary attitude toward the base band.

"We have some great musicians. About a month ago, we were playing for a parade over in San Angelo. And the gigantic Fifth Army Band was there, too. We looked like a little David beside the Goliath. We had our twenty-piece band and they must have had a hundred." Jim was obviously excited with his story. He talked fast and waved his arms around like a windmill. "But I told the guys to blow up a storm. And they did! The crowd cheered more for us than they did for that big ole army band. So we just played louder. I was real proud of 'em, General, they did us proud!"

"Boy, I love to hear stories like that, Jim." The General leaned back in his chair and chuckled at Jim's antics. Then he got quiet and lost his smile. "But I need to talk to you about something else. Could you close that door?" Jim got up and made sure the door was tightly closed. "I believe

Captain Juan Vasquez is your son-in-law, isn't he?"

"Yes, Sir, he sure is. We are really proud of him."

"And so are we, Jim, so are we. He is a great pilot and a fine instructor. But we have a small problem."

"What kind of problem?" Jim was obviously very concerned.

"Jim, as you know, the Armed Forces has a policy. Now, we know that these things happen. But we try to deal with them as best we can with as little fanfare as possible." The general was obviously uncomfortable with what he was trying to say.

"Just tell me what is going on, Sir."

"I don't know how to put this gently, Jim. Captain Vasquez has been seen engaging in – let's say –an intimate association – with –"

Jim jumped up out of his chair. "Is he messing around with some other woman? If he is I will kick his..."

The general interrupted. "No, Jim. I wish he were. We could handle that." The General forced a nervous laugh and groped for just the right words to ease the sting of what he was about to say. He finally spit out the sentence. "He is messing around with one of the *guys* –a flight instructor – in the Bachelor Officers Quarters!"

Jim's mouth fell open as he nearly fell down into his chair. He was speechless. He finally spoke under his breath. *"It's all starting to make sense, now."* Jim's thoughts were flashing back to some things Cali had been implying lately.

"What's that?"

"I - I'm sorry, sir. Nothing. Give me a minute to get my bearings."

"But all is not lost," the general quickly assured him. "I have a solution to this dilemma." The general took a deep breath and put his hands behind his head as he leaned back in his chair again. "As you know, we can't condone this kind of activity. Truth is, it's against the law. I am sure it goes on all the time here and there in the Armed Forces. But neither can we lose a good officer and a tremendous pilot if there is a solution. And I have a solution."

"I am up for anything, sir."

"Well, Jim, as much as I think of your abilities, this is not your problem. I only called you in here today as a friend. We have been pretty good friends for a long time."

Jim was proud of what he had just heard. He didn't think the base commander considered him as a personal friend. That was nice to know. "I only called you in here as a friend to give you a heads up about what I am going to do. You will not reveal this information to anyone, not even your wife, and *certainly* not to your daughter or Captain Vasquez. You will forget anything I have said when you leave this office. I must have your word on that!" Jim nodded his head in agreement. The general leaned toward Jim in confidence. "Have you seen those big black airplanes sitting on the flight line?" The General was speaking almost in a whisper.

"Well, sure. Everyone has. I heard someone say they maybe are some kind of 'spy planes' from England."

"Word gets around, doesn't it? Well, not exactly. I can't tell you all the details, but let us just say they are special airplanes for a special purpose. They will be flown from bases all over the world, including this one, on a mission that even I haven't been told all the details about. But we need to train a handful of pilots for this very special mission."

"I think I am ahead of you, General Bainbridge."

"I am sure you are, Jim. But, just to say it out loud, I am going to assign Captain Vasquez to the CIA, to train for this special mission. It is not

because of his 'problem,' Jim, 'cause he is a top
notch pilot, but it sure as hell kills two birds with
one stone, doesn't it?"

Chapter 41

Chui drifted off to sleep for a few minutes. He reached for his coffee cup but it was empty. Daylight was peeping into the motel window. He needed to get all his recollections together. The priest had promised him he would fill in some blanks in his life and he wanted to be ready with lots of questions. He wanted to recall everything about his mother. He had not seen her for years. *"Maybe she died. Someone would surely have told me. But where did she go and why?"* He needed answers to these questions. After all, these were some of the excuses he had used. He had rationalized that he had been abandoned by his mother. *"That was a really good reason to drink a lot."* He was chastising himself for his lame excuse. *"It was her fault, not mine."* He was purposefully sarcastic.

But try as he might, he simply did not remember much about that day. All he knew was, his mother took him to his grandparents, the William's, and kissed him goodbye and got into a car and drove away. She said she would be back soon, but she lied. She never came back.

His dad had gone on his "special mission" and had been gone for more than a year. He loved his grandparents dearly, but he missed his mom and his dad. And now they were both gone. Grandpa Vasquez reminded him that they would be coming back someday soon. But they didn't.

Neither one. He recalled that he must have been about eleven or so when his mother disappeared. Then there was the day they were informed that his father was a hero and was missing in action. He was proud of his father, but he somehow knew he would not ever see him again.

The fact is, Cali Vasquez was about to have a nervous breakdown. She knew her husband was gay. She knew the Air Force must have discovered that and sent him away to get rid of him. She had no idea where he went. And to top it all off, her best friend and wannabe lover was a priest and a drunk. And he was sent off somewhere, unknown to her, by the church, probably to dry out. Her mother was growing more and more distant from her. She was becoming more and more sarcastic and critical of her. Her life was a mess. She desperately wanted to be someone. She wanted to do something with her life. She had finished nearly two years of college courses at the University Of Wisconsin School Of Correspondence. She had excelled in every course she had taken. She was a brilliant student. The university had offered her a scholarship to come there and study, but she couldn't. She had responsibilities.

Paco, her father-in-law, was a total hypocrite. Two years ago he had been offered a deal by Art Gonzales, a local attorney, and the new owner of XERF, the radio station Paco had allegedly hated so much. Old Dr. Brinkley had died several years before but his reputation lived on. The radio station could sell nearly anything to the gullible people of the world, as long as it was couched in some sort of religious context. Art had called Paco one day and asked him if he had a few hundred acres of land he might devote to raising a new plant. He said it would be marketed as the elixir of life. It was a gift from God. It would heal anything by either rubbing it on or eating it. And it was an extremely prolific plant. It needed little water and would grow profusely in the hot Texas soil. Paco expressed an interest in this crop with a ready-made market. He would be paid handsomely for his crop. He decided to accept Art Gonzales's offer and hired several Mexicans and set out his crop of aloe vera. It made lots of money for him. The irony was, it really did cure lots of things. And, Paco suddenly decided the radio station that made his fence hum was not too bad after all.

The whole family was involved in the production of this new product. They were each given shares of stock in the company. The green leaves of aloe needed to be cleaned and processed and mixed with other herbs and whipped into a cream and put into a jar for distribution to the loyal listeners of XERF. It was marketed as a miracle from God, for $9.95 a jar. They received hundreds of thousands of orders from all over the world for this new aloe vera medical miracle. Cali was asked to help with the preparation of this new moneymaker. It was interfering with her studies, but she did her best to help out and was paid well and given a share of the business for her efforts.

But, still, she was not happy. This was not to be her life work. She had loftier goals to attain.

Then one day as she was approaching her twenty-ninth birthday, she snapped. She got up in the morning and went to her bank. She drew out all of the savings she and Johnny had accumulated. It was nearly $100,000. She gathered up all her clothes and secretly packed them into her car. She took her son to his grandparents and told them she needed to get away for a while. She wouldn't tell them where she was going. She said she didn't know. Then she left and headed for Florida.

The truth is, she did contact her parents and let them know she was OK. But try as they might, they could not convince her to come back to Texas. She would not tell them where she was, but she sounded healthy and contented. She asked them not to tell Chui anything about her. She thought it was better that way. She asked about Johnny and was told that he was missing in action. She cried when she heard that. She had always loved him and was terribly sad and sorry. She admitted to herself that she knew he was gay and they would never have had a normal marriage. When her family prodded her about what she was doing, she would say she was doing what she wanted to do for many years, but couldn't do it in Del Rio. They had no idea what she was talking about. She did not call often. And when she did, it was a very short conversation.

Chui grasped at the few memories his thoughts allowed him to have. He watched and waited for her to return for weeks and weeks. He cried himself to sleep at night for months. He finally immersed himself in his music and the memories of his mother and father began to fade. His grandparents were his parents now. He felt so lucky to have them, all four of them. He helped out with the aloe vera business and practiced his saxophone every day.

He dozed again. When he woke up it was daylight. He had had a busy night. His brain was tired. He had been through a lot of bad memories, but he needed to do that. It was morning and he was hungry. He got up and walked out the door and headed toward Denny's. As he passed the glass lobby door, he saw Punj sprucing up the area. He opened the door and shouted "Hey, Punj. Have you had breakfast?"

"No, not yet."

"Can you Hindu guys eat that crap at Denny's?"

"Sure, as long as it doesn't have any meat in it."

"Well, put out your no vacancy sign. I am buying you breakfast. I owe you, my friend. I owe you."

Punj laughed and grabbed his keys and locked the door. They broke bread together this Sunday morning.

Chapter 42

This cockpit was very small, compared to the other airplanes of the 60's. It was designed that way. It held only one person. There were lots of switches and dials and gauges for the lonely pilot to look over as he flew high above the earth. The wings were very large, almost like a glider. They were painted black. The entire plane was solid black and with as little as possible to attract the radar that might be searching for it. The mission of this plane was to shoot--not to shoot at anything but to shoot the earth below. It was loaded with cameras that could shoot high-resolution pictures from a great distance. The mission and the aircraft were both the highest top secret. Very few knew what was happening during this time when the cold war was at its peak. The Bay of Pigs invasion was as a result of pictures taken from this top-secret spy plane. Its nomenclature was not even known until Gary Powers was shot down while flying one over Russia. The CIA called it a "U-2."

On this particular night, Major Juan Vasquez had been somewhere over Siberia in Northern Russia, miles above the earth, shooting his pictures for the CIA and thinking. He thought about his wife and son. He thought about his mother and father. He wondered what they might be doing right this moment. He was especially lonely this night. It was Christmas time and that meant the ranch would be decorated and lights would be placed all around the big front gate. There would be gifts and food. The Williams's would be invited over. Jim and his dad would be having their friendly but adversary discussions about politics. They would have a couple of drinks. Momma Randa would probably have made some pasole and maybe even some fresh handmade tortillas. Sister Maria might be there. She was far too pretty and talented to have become a nun. But it was her life. She had been a nun for a few years now. Since she spoke fluent Spanish, she served at a mission in Mexico. Johnny hoped she could get away and attend the festivities. He remembered the old days when he was young. He wished he could be there, too.

Ramon and Damon, his twin brothers, were both in a place now known to the world as a controversial war zone. It was called Viet Nam. They were sent there as "advisers." But, more and more U S military personnel had been dispersed to that problem area. Johnny was afraid his brothers were soon to be in harm's way. He was proud of them. Neither of the twins had gotten married. The "Corps" was their life and wives simply did not fit that lifestyle. He said a little prayer for them on this Christmas Day.

He tried not to think about his son. But it was unavoidable. He missed Chui, more than anyone could imagine. He knew he would be the one who suffered the most from this mess. He was such a good boy and such a fabulous musician. His grandfather, Jim, was an excellent teacher. Chui was twelve – exactly twelve -- today – or tomorrow – or yesterday. He didn't know which time zone he was in. He was so grateful that Chui had such good grandparents. He needed them. He needed them very much. He hoped that Chui's life was not so terribly disrupted with his dad's problems. He hoped he did not know about his dad's problems. He hoped he was OK.

Then, there was his beautiful Caliente. He so wished that things could have been different. He was not cruel to her. Not on purpose. He didn't mean to be. But he was simply not interested in her sexually. He knew he was the envy of every boy in his class -- every boy in the whole school -- every boy who ever laid eyes on her! But he had always been attracted to boys. He had always been that way, but he couldn't admit that to anyone. He was a very good actor. He could put on a good show. He thought he should pick the most gorgeous girl in the school. Maybe he might change. Maybe he could start to be attracted to girls if he just could have a nice sexy girlfriend. He tried. God knows how hard he tried. But it just never happened. He just could not change what was. He had to get away from everyone and concentrate on being the best pilot he could be.

The big black U-2 droned on. It was a quiet, smooth running and very fast aircraft. It did its job efficiently and effectively. Major Vasquez had to reach above his O2 mask and wipe a tear from his eyes under his shield. He glanced down and automatically swiped his vision across the gauges to make sure his cameras were functioning properly. They were.

Then his thoughts began to focus on Rob -- Captain Robin Vanstreen. He had been a flight instructor at Laughlin. He had grown up in Michigan, and had been in the Air Force for eight years. After he enlisted, he applied for OCS and then was accepted into flight school. They were nearly complete opposites. Rob was from pure white Dutch ancestry. Johnny was pure Mexican. Neither man intended to have things happen the way they did. But when one finds a friend who has the same interests -- at least the same... Major Vasquez paused and thought to himself. *"Here's the deal. You are flying about ten miles above the earth over Russia. You are a spy for the United States of America, working for the CIA. You are all alone and if you get shot down or even have engine problems, or have to land for any reason – no one will claim you. No one will help you. No one will rescue you. If ever anyone in the world was on his own – you are, ole buddy. You are way up here ON YOUR OWN. So this is no time to be bullshitting yourself. Right now it is time for pure, simple honesty! You and Rob were looking for each other. You found each other. You either fell in love or lust, or something. But it was a wonderful relationship. You both just got carried away and got caught!! It shouldn't have to be that way. But it is. You both knew the risks. You just flat ass got caught!"*

He never knew what happened to Rob. But, he suddenly resigned his commission. He wondered why *he* had gotten such a deal and Rob had not. He knew that his father-in-law was pretty close with the old man, the general. He wondered if Jim had any influence in this situation. He thought he probably did. He wasn't sure if that was good or not. It shouldn't have to be that way. It wasn't fair. But the world is not a fair place. If it were, he wouldn't have been cursed with this sexual preference problem. "Fag - Queer." Those were the unkind terms used for men like this. "Gay." That was the new word. That was the kinder way of saying it. That was the acceptable way of saying "homosexual."

His nightly mission was about completed. He had relaxed a little and nearly lulled himself to sleep far above the Siberian tundra and was about to return to his base to turn in his film. He was suddenly jerked into reality. His radar started beeping incessantly. There was something on his tail. It was a frightening sound. This was the first time he had been tracked since he began these CIA spy missions and for a split second he didn't quite know how to react. Then his intensive training took over and he instinctively headed for cover. He put his big black aircraft into a steep dive and immediately dropped down about five thousand feet. He made a swift bank to the left, and at full speed headed for the nearest friendly sky.

"That was a close one." He spoke out loud into his O2 mask. "I think they have found me -- must have been a missile. It doesn't matter what it was, it knows I am up here. I sure don't want to have the same fate as Gary Powers." He vectored his way back toward the nearest friendly territory. He had been making these dangerous but important missions for about two years. He had long since lost count. He had never been discovered – until now. Major Vasquez was having a very significant argument with himself as he drew a long breath and tried to think straight. He had just made a very narrow escape. He was not ready to die.

There are times when a life-changing decision must be made instantly, without forethought – an "epiphany." This was one of those moments. Maybe it was because it was Christmas. He had one last flash of his life before him as he checked his altitude. He had been dropping rapidly for several minutes. He had apparently avoided the Russian missile. But he knew there would be more missiles. He was low enough now. He should be right on the border, just into Finland. He set the autopilot on a course that would eventually send his multi-million dollar U-2 right into the Arctic Ocean. He crossed himself and reached up for the lever that would cause his canopy to disappear into the night – and the next split second would catapult him into the sky. It was December. There would be no daylight to speak of this time of year in northern Finland. He hoped he was going to land in Finland. He was pretty sure his instruments were correct. The moon had just come up over the horizon and now he could see the white covered ground below pretty well. He had his hand on the canopy release, but as he tightened his glove-covered fingers around it he took a last look through the cockpit windshield. *"I can't believe this. It must be a miracle! It looks like a runway down there."* Major Vasquez was staring at the ground about two thousand feet below and about two miles ahead of him. The moon was not playing tricks on him. It was a very long snow-covered white strip of land, high in the mountains of what he hoped was Finland. *"If I could just land this bird instead of dunking it into the ocean. Let me just get a little closer and have a better look. I wonder if it's long enough? It sure looks like it. I wonder how smooth it is? It isn't going to matter much if I don't make up my mind pretty fast!"* He lined up the big black airplane and sized up the situation. It was a wide shelf on the side of a mountain. If he could carry this off, it would give him a place to camp out until he got his bearings. If he didn't, it wouldn't matter, would it? Although he had been trained to survive, this would be a lot better than just landing in this bitter Arctic cold with nothing but a parachute and a few survival tools in his pocket. The point of no return was approaching pretty fast. He was going about two hundred miles per hour about now. He dropped his gear and pulled on every lever and pushed every button that would slow the big aircraft to a more manageable speed as he cut his engine and began to drift down the last couple of hundred feet. The Major was using every morsel of training and experience he had gained in his years of flying. He saw the ground coming up at him at a terrific rate of speed as he pulled back and let the heavy plane stall out at the exact precise split second. The plane hit and bounced and bounced again and again as its pilot hung on for dear life. He allowed as how this must have been the roughest landing he had ever made, including his first day of flying school. The snow was flying from both sides. He was plowing a ditch in the snow the Minnesota Highway Department would be proud of. He watched the trees fly by like fence posts on a super highway in Germany. Brakes were useless on the slick cliff, and so he continued to hang on for what seemed like hours as the plane finally began to lose its speed and slow down. It finally came to a stop in the high mountains of Finland.

Chapter 43

The Sunday morning church crowd had not yet arrived at Denny's. The Mexican guy and the guy with the white turban sitting together having breakfast attracted their share of glances. Chui and Punj had ordered their respective fare. Chui was eating his eggs and toast with grits and bacon. Punj got the same sans the bacon. They both had coffee. It was Chui who spoke first. "It could be my imagination, but you seem to know Frank pretty well. I mean, I get the idea you knew our priest friend before I came along."

Punj grinned, showing his white teeth under his black beard. "Wellll." He dragged out the word as if he were giving himself a little time to configure his words just the right way so as not to lie but also not to divulge more information than he should. "I have attended his church."

"You what? I thought you were a Hindu."

"I am. But I guess one could say I am a *liberal* Hindu. My family has been in the United States for several years. My father is – let us say – doesn't go hungry."

"You trying to tell me he is rich?"

"Yes. More or less. He has financed my purchase of some properties in the US. I have two brothers. Two of us have motels and the other one is a doctor in Tucson. But – back to your question – You see, just because I am a Hindu and our beliefs do not include the use of alcohol – doesn't mean some of us didn't get – lets say – 'Americanized' in our youth and strayed now and then. Let me just say I met Frank at a meeting and let it go at that.

"I get the picture. No need to go into detail." Chui paused and took a big bite of his toast. "So you knew more about me than you let on? You should get into acting."

"Don't make me tell you more than I should," Punj grinned through his beard again. "I will say this. You were pretty easy. I just dropped my business card in your case while you were playing on the corner, and you took the bait, as you Americans say. You came right over here and checked in." Punj's eyes sparkled as he spoke with his dialect.

"Well, you certainly were a good actor. You acted like you never saw me before in your life when I came into your motel on Friday." Chui chided his breakfast partner. "What would have happened if I hadn't just come over here and checked in?"

"We had a plan B."

"We? You mean you and that frigging priest?"

"Yep -- Frank and I had a plan B. He was following you and making sure you went in the right direction – toward my motel. If you went into the wrong one, he was going to – how do you Americans say it – shortstop you, somehow – get you back on the track. But – no mattah – you played the game just like we planned. I sure hope I am not telling something you are not supposed to know!" Punj looked a little concerned.

"Well now. You guys think you are pretty slick, don't you?" Chui feigned an angry face and then grinned. "What else can you tell me?"

"Nothing! I have told you too much already."

"How about those robes you stole from the Hilton in Chicago?"

Punj had just taken a big drink of coffee. He spit it out all over the table. "That is TOP secret. I will NEVER discuss that any further." He laughed so loud he attracted the attention of the entire restaurant.

"You still haven't told me how you got to know Frank."

"As I said, I met him at a meeting. We struck up a conversation and he invited me to his church. He told me there would be no attempt to convert me. I didn't have to do any of the stuff – you know – the communion, the kneeling and that sort of thing. I could just come and sit and be among friends and continue to have my own beliefs. And so I did. I'm still a Hindu but I go to his church sometimes. It's a wonderful arrangement."

"We have known each other for a couple of years now. After a while, you begin to feel more comfortable with a new friend. I began to tell him more about my life and he told me about his. Sometimes one can begin to get to the bottom of one's problems and what causes one to do some of the things one does." Punj was twirling his index finger around in a circle in the air as he spoke, trying to be intellectually evasive. "I suppose we know quite a lot about each other. Father Frank is a good friend."

"He certainly has been good to me." Chui suddenly got serious. "You know he knew me when I was very young – in Del Rio, Texas. That is where I grew up." Chui paused for several seconds. Punj waited for him to continue. "I was pretty young, but I remember that he left town suddenly and unexpectedly. My mother was very, very upset. My dad had joined the Air Force and was a pilot. He was sent on what was called a 'special mission.' I think I was about ten – maybe younger – I don't remember. Then a few months later my mother left. She said she was going to get away for a while – but she never came back." Chui was rambling on -- getting a bit emotional with his story. "But – I don't want to bore you with my trials and tribulations. That was a long, long time ago. She might have died by now. I haven't seen her for many years. My grandparents were wonderful to me. They sent me to North Texas and I got my degree in music. Then I became a professional musician – did some recording – played with some pretty well-known bands – played in California for several years – got into the sauce – and you know the rest." Chui hastened the end to his story so as not to bore his new friend. Punj nodded his head unconsciously, as though he already knew.

"Frank has not told me much about his early life." Punj broke the silence as they finished their food and sipped on their refills. "I do know he became an alcoholic at a pretty young age and spent a lot of time in Santa Fe, then was eventually sent here to El Paso." Punj paused, as though he might say too much if he went on.

"I am going to meet with him later today. Maybe I can fill you in on the blanks." Chui welcomed the lighter mood of the conversation.

"Guess I had better get back to my little ole motel. My wife has been holding down the fort, as you Americans say."

Chui grabbed the two tickets and paid the tabs. Punj left a nice tip for the waitress. The two men walked out and headed back toward the Motel 6 next door. Punj unlocked the door. Chui told him he had enjoyed their little breakfast together and hoped they could do it again sometime soon. Punj acknowledged and went inside. Chui unlocked the door to 108 and went inside. His message light was flashing. He picked up the phone and punched the "0" button. "Do I have a message?"

"Yep. Frank called. He left a number. He wants you to call him back A-S-A-P, as you Americans say."

Chapter 44

1961. Highway 90 was the road from Del Rio to San Antonio. Cali's white Ford full of clothes and belongings was traveling east. She was gulping deep breaths as she managed to keep the car in its proper lane. She had just told her parents and her only son goodbye. She had no idea where she was going or why she desperately needed to leave, but nonetheless, here she was trying to see the road through tears that didn't seem to stop. She finally reached a small rest area. *"Oh Lord. It's the same place Johnny stopped when he brought me back from that God-awful place in Uvalde before Chui was born."* She realized where she was and pulled over and turned off the ignition. Tears were streaming down her cheeks as she sobbed and sobbed for several minutes. "I should turn around and go back." But she needed to re-read the letter that had been taped to her door a few days ago. She had no idea how it got there. She needed to be sure it was not a dream. It was from Johnny. He was supposedly "missing in action," but, several days ago, here came this letter. Those two things did not add up. She had read the letter dozens of times but desperately needed to read it just once more, just to be sure it was real. That letter was the final straw that led her to decide to leave. She wanted to be sure.

She opened up the well-worn envelope, pulled out the hand-written paper and read it once again:

My darling and precious Caliente,

I have so much to tell you. I must try and make you understand as best I can. First and more importantly, you must understand that you are such a total feminine woman, such a sensuous being, such a wonderful, normal person. No problem we ever had was even remotely your fault. You were perfect. It was I who had the problem.

You must have realized long ago that I was not a normal male. I am a homosexual. As much as I tried to deny it and as much as I tried to become normal, it was just not to be.

When you discovered you were pregnant with Chui, I was so happy. I just knew that would change me and I would be normal. But that didn't happen. I love Chui as much as any father could. I want you to know that.

I did love you very much, in my limited way. The few times we had sex were dismal failures, I think you know that. I desperately wanted to make love to you, but I simply could not do it. My mind was on men I had known. No, I did not cheat on you. I only cheated in my mind. That was true for several years. But then, I met someone who felt the same way as I did. His name is Rob. We will let it go at that

199

for now. My parents know nothing about my problem. I must keep it that way. Our religion does not allow homosexuals. My mother might accept it, but my father would not know how to deal with it.

I am sure your father had something to do with my reassignment. Rob was not so lucky to have such a wonderful father-in-law. He was asked to resign his commission. I do not know what became of him. If I get through this assignment, I hope to find him some day.

Please know that I love you deeply —but only as a friend – not as a wife or lover. I hope we can see each other someday, but I do not know what sort of turn my life might take just now. I have this strong premonition that things might go badly for me someday soon. It is an intense feeling. That is the main reason for writing this letter to you. After the proper period of time, you can legally remarry. I hope you will and find happiness. You must not tell anyone about this correspondence. It could endanger my life and the lives of several others. It could even have worldwide consequences. I trust you implicitly. Otherwise I would not have taken the chance of writing to you. Please destroy this letter after you read it.

You may not hear from me for a very long time, if ever. Please give Chui an extra special kiss for me. I wish you could tell him whom the kiss is from. Maybe someday you can.

I cannot tell you where I am or what I am doing. Some very special people took a big chance to get this letter to you. I cannot ask them to do it again.

I love all of you more than you can ever know. I wish you could convey that to our wonderful family, but you must not.

Be happy and be safe.

Juanito

Cali held the letter close to her heart. Then she returned it to its envelope and put it in her purse. She kept it, but never read it again.

She now knew what she had to do. She dried her eyes and wiped her nose with her sleeve, then restarted the white Ford. Uvalde would be next -- Then on to San Antonio, Houston and points east. She now knew where she was going. She would head for the place she loved the most, Fort Walton Beach, Florida. She clenched her teeth and wiped her eyes. Her own voice bounced off the windshield as she said out loud to herself, "Caliente Suzanne Williams Vasquez, it is time for you to stop being the spoiled brat you have been all your life and *grow up*. Go do what you must do.

Do something for someone other than yourself. Become someone. Whatever it takes – become someone! Make a contribution to the world!" Her voice was growing louder and more resolute and made her begin to smile as she pounded her hand on the steering wheel. At last she had a sense of purpose and calmness. She had a plan and was about to put it into action.

Chapter 45

Chui memorized the phone number Punj had just given him. He pressed the 9 on the phone and dialed the number.

"Father Frank."

"Hey Frank, this is Chui."

"Hey. Amigo mio. Como estas? How would you like to take a little viaje up to Santa Fe?" Frank did not often speak Spanish, although he was fluent.

"New Mexico?" Chui asked the redundant question.

"Yeah. It's only a couple of hours, maybe three. There is a jam session on Sunday afternoon at the La Fonda. A lot of the guys I played with are always there. We'll have a great time. What do you think? You up for it?"

"Seguro que si," Chui answered back in Spanish. "Hell yes, as long as you do the driving. I might catch a little nap. I had a hard night."

"Yeah, several of us did, thanks to you, you little shit."

"That ain't no way for no preacherman to talk. I will be here waiting."

"You might as well check out. Bring all your stuff and we will put it in the car."

"I travel lightly. I don't have much to bring – just my trusty ole sax and a handful of clothes. I'll go say goodbye to Punj and see ya in a few minutes."

"I'll be there."

Thirty minutes later Frank pulled up to the motel. He knocked on the door to room 108. He was dressed in a bright red shirt and yellow slacks. "Where the hell did you get that outfit?" Chui kidded the priest.

"These are my jam session clothes, man. I wear those drab black clothes all the time. So, I like to dress like this when I go to Santa Fe."

"I would say you got them at the thrift store, but they probably throw clothes like that in the trash." Frank laughed and told Chui to get in before he drove off without him for making such disrespectable remarks about his wardrobe. The two men were obviously becoming great friends and could jive each other. Chui opened the back door and threw his blue overcoat, a stack of clothes and his saxophone in the back seat. They headed onto I-10 and up toward Las Cruses and onto I-25 toward Albuquerque and Santa Fe, New Mexico.

I-25 north of Las Cruces runs parallel to and west of the Rio Grande River, past T or C, as the locals call Truth or Consequences. The interstate is surrounded by mountains and canyons, causing a giant roller-coaster ride. It lulled Chui to sleep for a while. "There is Caballo Lake." Frank's voice caused Chui to jerk his head as though he had been awake all along. "Sorry. I didn't mean to wake you."

"I wasn't asleep. Just resting my eyes."

"I heard that story before. Well, now that you are awake, tell me what you have been doing for the last 20 years."

"I don't think we have enough time."

"We have about two hours to go. That should be enough."

"Well, OK. Chui laid his head back, put his hands behind his neck and looked up at the headliner of the car. "Where shall I start? How about after college?" Chui began his life story and Frank listened quietly but intensely. "I graduated from North Texas with a degree in music. I think you knew that." Frank nodded. "But I took a minor in business. Grandpa Vasquez had started that aloe vera business for that radio station and it was going extremely well. He had gotten together with some lady from down in the valley, near Harlingen, and they came up with an aloe cream. It had all sorts of herbs and things in it – in

205

addition to the aloe. One of the ingredients was sesame. So they called it 'Open Sesame,' after the fairy tale. People were sending their five bucks for this stuff from all over the world. Everyone was making money hand over fist." Chui spoke the last few words through a gigantic yawn.

"Am I boring you?" Frank chided him for his yawn.

"Sorry -- just relaxing a little."

"Go ahead. So the aloe biz was making you a lot of money. What about your music?"

"Well, Grandpa Williams took care of that. I was playing in his band at Jack's and a few other places around the area. It was a great life."

"Is that when the – uh – booze ---?"

Chui interrupted. "That started in college. Just a few beers and some wine. That wasn't enough so the hard stuff was faster – Hell – why am I telling you – you know the drill."

"Yep – sure do. But I wasn't trying to be sarcastic. I knew I had a problem. But I wouldn't admit it. Did that happen to you?

"I honestly don't remember. I think it sort of sneaked up on me. I know I was working lots of hours. All day I was overseeing that aloe business and playing at night. And finally one day a band came through town. You know, one of those 'territory' bands that tours around the country? Anyway, they were playing at the Del Rio Country Club. It was 'Chet Parsons and the Saints.' I remember it well. They needed a drummer."

"A drummer? That's not your ax."

"I do have a degree in music from one of the best music schools in the country, you know. I could play drums well enough for a Mickey Mouse band. They had called Grandpa at the base band office and asked if he had a drummer they could borrow for the night. Grandpa volunteered me. He thought I could use the experience. It was no big deal – just play like it was Guy Lombardo or Lawrence Welk." They both laughed.

"Yeah, I have been there a few times myself," Frank sympathized. "So you played drums with Parsons and the Saints."

"I did. But everyone on the band drank their brains out before the gig. I thought this was really great. So I joined in. I guess I thought it was part of the deal. We even smoked a joint or two during intermission. After the job, Chet asked me if I wanted to go on the road with them for a while. I said I didn't want to play drums but I would play sax. He had three tenors and so he fired one of them and hired me."

"On the spot?"

"On the spot. I got on the bus and left that night after the gig. I was drunk as a skunk. I was about twenty-three then. I thought this would be my big break. Grandpa was so pissed at me. But I told him it was his fault – he got me the job-- and to leave me alone. I told him I didn't have any parents and so no one could tell me what to do. After I sobered up, I called him later and apologized. By that time we were in Omaha."

"Holy Shit, Son. What a way to start your life."

"Well, it did get better. I stayed with Chet for about three months and learned to drink and stand up at the same time. He finally fired me after I called him a drunken asshole. He stumbled into the bass drum one night in Bakersfield, I think it was. The bus was parked right behind the door to the stage. He was in the bus having his five or nine drinks before the job. He staggered out of the bus and right through the stage door and onto the bandstand. He couldn't get stopped and smacked into the drums and almost knocked them off the stage. But, somehow, he grabbed the mike stand, pulled himself up and played the job, just like a drunken trouper. After the job, I told him he was a drunken asshole. He fired me and then a half hour later asked me to come back."

Frank began to laugh like a crazy man at that story. "So what did you do?"

"I hopped a bus to LA and looked for a job there. Funny thing. I went over to Hermosa Beach. They had some little joints there on the beach. It was Sunday afternoon and some guys were jamming. They were playing some great jazz. I asked if I could sit in and they said sure, but just a couple of tunes. I know you know the deal. That is an excuse to get rid of you if you can't cut it." Frank nodded in agreement. "Well, I played all afternoon and into the evening. One of the guys was playing with Stan Kenton at the time, believe it or not."

"You mean THE Stan Kenton?"

"The very one. He was on tour at the time and needed a 4th tenor just for a few weeks. They had some proms booked at some colleges. Anyway, I went over and auditioned. Stan's music director did the audition, Stan wasn't even there. But they hired me. I played in Illinois and Indiana and up in Minnesota. They used several pickup musicians like me. No one knew the difference. It sounded the same. But ole Stan was always there. He was a real sweetheart."

"Did you stay ---"?

"You bet I stayed sober. Probably the longest time ever. Doesn't mean I didn't have a few after hours. But during the gig – no drinking. That was some damn fine music. But it was over in a couple of months. They went back to LA to do some recording and didn't need me."

"Sure looks good on your resume."

"It looked so good, it got me some good gigs. No big names, but a lot of work. It started my career. I did a lot of studio work in LA, just backup for some wannabe singers, no one especially famous. That lasted for several years. I could make big bucks for a few days and then drink for a while. But I managed to stay sober enough when I needed to."

Frank and Chui rode along I-25, through the New Mexico hills and canyons. They had passed Caballo Lake and then on past Elephant Butte Lake. There was nothing much said for half an hour or so.

Chui had dozed off and Frank let him sleep for a while. Chui finally jerked his head and woke up, embarrassed that he had fallen asleep. "Sorry. I didn't mean to poop out."

"That's OK. We are coming up to Socorro. We are about an hour or so from Albuquerque. You want to stop for some coffee? I could probably use some gas and a pee anyway."

"Sounds like a winner. You must know this road pretty well."

"I have driven it a few hundred times. I get up to Santa Fe quite regularly. Remember, I lived up there for a few years. I probably drive up here a couple of times a month. I have lots of friends in Santa Fe. I want you to meet some of them."

The car pulled off the exit and stopped at a Circle K. Both men got out and stretched. Frank filled up the car with gas and went to the bathroom while Chui got two cups of coffee and paid for them. "Coffee is on me."

The car sped back on to the interstate and headed back to the North toward Santa Fe. "You said you wanted me to meet your friends in Santa Fe. Are these guys musicians?"

"Some of them. Some are people I have known for a long time -- old friends who helped me out when I needed it. You'll see when we get there."

Chapter 46

"Hello." The voice on the phone sounded a bit apprehensive.

"Is this General John Bainbridge?"

"Who's calling?"

"I'm sorry, I should have identified myself. This is Jim Williams. I knew General Bainbridge when he was at Laughlin Air Base. Do I have the right number?"

"God damn, Jim. Hell yes, this is John Bainbridge. How the hell are you? I haven't heard from you for years."

"Yes, Sir. I know. It has been awhile."

"Jim, lets cut out the 'sir' stuff and the 'General' stuff. I am retired now and so are you. We are old friends. Please just call me 'John.' I would feel more comfortable."

"That's fine with me, Gen – uh John." Jim found it difficult to be quite so familiar with his old commander. "Where are you now? This phone number I got from the base is a Florida area code."

"That's right. I retired in Florida at a place called 'Bird Key.' It's just outside Sarasota. Lots of military people have retired here. It's pretty nice -- right on the Gulf. It's all gated and sealed off from the rest of the world -- keeps the riff-raff out!" The general belted out a laugh and Jim joined in. "What about you, Jim? Where did you end up after our little stint in the Texas desert?"

"I moved to New Orleans, Sir – uh John. I have been playing with a great group of guys here. We play in a joint in the Quarter. You know I have always loved to play Dixieland and now I get to play it all the time."

"You know, Jim, you won't believe this. I played the trumpet years ago. I think I told you. Well, I got that old moldy horn out a few years ago and started playing again. We have a bunch of guys here in Sarasota who get together a couple of times a month. It's a little jazz club. We aren't too good, but we have a great time. And it gets me out of the house and out of my wife's hair." He laughed again. "How about your wife, what is her name?"

"Susie. Her name is Susie."

"That's right. How is she?"

"Not too well, John. She is in a nursing home. She has Alzheimer's. She doesn't know me anymore,"

"My God, Jim. I am so sorry. That is such sad news."

"Well, I am dealing with it." Jim paused for a few seconds. "I need to ask you a big favor, John."

"Sure, Jim. Anything. What do you need?"

"Do you remember my son-in-law, Johnny Vasquez? We had an issue—"

"Of course, I remember. It was one of the most difficult things I ever had to do. I understand he is Missing in Action. The Russians reported that his plane was shot down over Siberia. But they never produced anything. They said they never found the plane. No one knows what really happened to him."

"John, can you tell me the man he was involved with? You told me it was a fellow instructor, but you didn't tell me who it was. And can you tell me what happened to him?"

The general was silent for several seconds. He cleared his throat and finally spoke. "Jim. I don't know how much clout I have these days. This is probably classified." The general paused for a couple of seconds, and then he spoke. "If you can give me an hour or so, I will find out everything I can. Give me your phone number and I will call you back as soon as I find out."

Jim Williams was excited for the first time in a long time. He gave John Bainbridge his phone number and thanked him profusely.

He paced around his living room with his hands behind his back. What seemed like a day was only about two hours. Finally, the phone rang. "Hello, Jim Williams."

"I have your information. The boy's name was Robin
Vanstreen. He was asked to resign his commission. He went to Michigan. That was his home. You got a pencil? Here is his address and everything I could find out."

The general read Rob's entire dossier to Jim as he frantically wrote it down. "General, uh John -- I can't thank you enough."

"Jim. I will not ask you what you need this information for. I don't care. I will ask you to do the same thing as I asked you all those years ago. We will not mention this ever again. Please forget where you got this stuff. My conversation with you today was just two old Air Force buddies checking up on each other. Understood?"

"Yes sir, General Bainbridge. I got it, loud and clear. Thank you, thank you. You have a good day and enjoy your Florida sunshine, and don't play too many blue notes on your trumpet. Good to talk with you after all these years." Jim hung up the phone.

Chapter 47

Frank's car wheeled back on to Interstate 25. The two men sipped their coffee in silence for a few minutes. "What about your grandparents?"

"As far as I know, my Grandmother Vasquez is still alive. Grandpa died several years ago. I was playing somewhere in California. By the time I found out, the funeral was over. He was not very forgiving of my lifestyle. He was pretty set in his ways, a typical Hispanic – you know – very macho and kind of a control freak. I don't mean to be disrespectful. But, I sort of fell out of favor with him. As a matter of fact, he more or less *disowned* me. But Abuela Randa – we were good buddies – especially when Paco was not around. I called and told her how sad I was. I explained that I didn't know about Paco's death until after the funeral. She understood. She always understood. She was a real saint. She must be close to a hundred by now. I sure hope she is alive and well."

"How about your mother's parents?"

"Grandpa Jim and Grandma Susie? That is a long sad story. But I guess we aren't going anywhere for a while, are we?" Chui closed his eyes as if he was bringing up some faraway memories. "After I went to California, I came back to visit once in awhile. Grandma Susie was such a good mother to me. She put up with so much crap. I owe her so much. I could never repay her. But, she began to get forgetful. Not too noticeable – just a little at a time. Grandpa took her to the base hospital to have her checked out. They said it was just a sign of getting old and forgetful and not to worry about it." Chui stopped talking and stared out the window for a while. "But it got worse and worse. She began to get cruel and spiteful. They called it 'dementia.' Today we call it Alzheimer's." His voice cracked with emotion as he related the story.

"Grandpa Jim was ready to retire. They had planned to move to New Orleans and buy a little house. Grandpa loved Dixieland music and there is no better place than the Big Easy to play Dixieland."

Frank's mind drifted away for a few seconds. He curled his lips and secretly brushed a tear away at the thought of his dear old friend with such a terrible disease. He recalled that night on the beach. His mind wandered back to Padre Island. He was so young then. He came very close to taking advantage of Susie while she was drunk on wine. He remembered that she was so very tempting, lying there on the blanket, wearing just her swimsuit and a sweatshirt. It took all the will power he could muster to keep his composure, but he *did*. He was finally able to get her up, he remembered, and somehow got her into the top bunk in their little cabana. He covered her up and returned to the beach to check on all the kids. His thoughts were racing as Chui's voice faded in the background. He remembered he could smell something pungent -- like weeds burning -- as he approached the campfire. He was so naïve; he didn't know what it was back then. The four boys who came to visit had jumped up as he walked toward the group. They disappeared down the beach. But many of the others were obviously under the influence of something. Especially Cali, he remembered. She was lying there, all wrapped up around Johnny. He walked up and surprised them and they both jumped up. Cali was crying – She had taken off her swimsuit top. He pulled her aside and tried to talk to her ---

"They had planned on this life for so long. But Grandma just kept on fading away. She couldn't remember much of anything." Chui's voice faded Frank back to the present. "I went down to New Orleans a few times and visited them. I played with some of Grandpa's musician friends. It was like he had died and gone to heaven. He loved that music so much and played it so well. Grandma lasted for a few years, but finally had to go live in a home. Grandpa Jim was so good to her. He would visit her every day and talk to her. But she didn't know who he was. She didn't know who I was, either. She finally died. It was a blessing, but after that, Grandpa Jim was never the same. I stayed with him for a few days after the funeral." Chui twisted around in his seat and looked into the back seat. "You saw that old blue overcoat I wear?"

Frank nodded his head. "Yeah. It is pretty well worn."

"Well, I was looking at some stuff in the shed where Grandpa Jim lived and found his old uniforms stored away. I saw that overcoat hanging there with all the stripes on the sleeves. I asked him if I could have it since I was going to be in cold weather now and then. It was nearly new, he had hardly worn it and, besides, he got a new one when he became an officer. He told me to go ahead and take it but I needed to cut off the stripes. I have worn it ever since. It makes me feel close to him. He lived for just a couple of years, and then he died, too. I think it was from a broken heart."

Frank was dead silent. "I am so sorry, Son. It must have been a terrible loss for you."

"They had an old fashioned New Orleans funeral for him," Chui went on. "It was so great. It all began in an old church. I think it was a Baptist church. Nearly everyone was black. He was laid out on the little stage and the band was there to play. They had placed his trumpet in his hand as though he was ready to play in the heavenly jazz band. They played 'Mine Eyes Have Seen the Glory of the Comin' of the Lord.' You know how they do it -- real slow for the first chorus? Then take the tempo up a notch and make it really swing." Chui snapped his fingers as though he was playing along. "Then they talked and laughed about Grandpa, then they 'Amen'ed' a little and played some more spirituals. It was like a show. It was so fantastic. I was just fine until they told the mourners that they were going to play one last special song just for 'Brother Jim, to send him on his way.' Then they played a wonderful Dixieland version of 'Back Home Again in Indiana.' That is where Grandpa was born, you know. Anyway, that just about did me in. I couldn't hold it any longer." Chui began to sob, uncontrollably, at the recollection, as the tears streamed down his cheeks. Frank was politely silent as they drove on for a few miles.

"They carried his casket down the street to the cemetery. The band played 'Just a Closer Walk with Thee'." Chui could hardly talk as he recalled this memory. He regained his composure again. "They played it real slow on the way to the cemetery. The group sort of marched real slow and swayed with the music. When they got there, a black preacher said some wonderful things about Grandpa. The ladies were all dressed in black. I saw one lady standing way in the back, near the trees. She had on a long black dress with a veil over her face. I couldn't tell who she was. I always wondered if it was my mother. She disappeared before I could find out."

Chui pondered this thought for a few seconds. "Then on the way back, they played the song a little faster, then a little faster and finally got it up to tempo. Then they switched to 'Didn't He Ramble.' Everyone danced and rejoiced at Jim's passing. It was perfect. It was exactly as he

220

would have wanted. It was a wonderful ceremony. I will never forget it. It was one of the highlights of my life."

After a few minutes, Frank broke the silence. "Chui." He said quietly, "I grew up in New Orleans. I have seen that many times and each one is special. Your Grandpa was given a very special tribute by his friends and fellow musicians. Very few white men get that honor. You can be so very proud of him." Frank's words were exactly what Chui needed to hear.

"Only bad thing about it was – I went back to his house and got drunk for a whole week. I have no idea what happened to his stuff. I woke up on a bus in California. I am not sure I have been completely sober since then -- until last Friday."

They headed for Santa Fe and remained silent for a long time.

Chapter 48

It was 1961. Cali Vasquez parked her white Ford along the curb at the edge of Fort Walton Beach. It did not look the same. Lots of new businesses had been built and opened. Nothing looked familiar. She had looked forward to this minute for the last fourteen years but it was so anti-climatic. The sand was there and the surf was still the same. She had the horrible feeling that she had made a gigantic mistake. But she squared her jaw and gritted her teeth and walked over to the water's edge. She had removed her shoes and was holding them over her shoulder as she walked along the surf. She had on peddle-pushers. The cool, salty water washed up around her feet. *"Well, it's too late now. Here I am, for better or worse. I can't turn back now. I have made my bed and I am going to lie in it."*

Her thoughts went to her parents and parents-in-law. She prayed that they would someday forgive her. But most of all, she prayed that her son would someday understand. She wished Father Francisco would suddenly appear. She desperately needed to talk to him. She had been thinking about him for the past three days as she drove across Texas, and especially as she passed the highway to New Orleans. She thought about stopping there for a few days, but decided that was not the thing to do. She thought maybe he was there. She never knew where he was sent after his dismissal from the church and sudden departure.

She desperately wished that her dear friend had taken up a different vocation. She knew he felt the same way. He had never said it in so many words, but she knew. Several times when he had a drink or two too many, he made some fairly obvious advances toward her. As a matter of fact, he had been pretty direct about it. Cali grinned as she thought of the few times she had to fend him off in his office. It was not easy to turn him down. He could be so charming and desirable. She could have given in so easily. But she didn't.

The sand felt warm under her feet. *"There is no place in the world like the Florida west coast with sand like this. It's like sugar."* She walked along the beach for about an hour, then returned to her car and headed south toward Tampa Bay.

Her destination --The University of South Florida. She stopped at an inexpensive motel close by, checked in and changed her clothes. Next stop was the first bank she saw. It was the First National Bank of Florida. She went inside and opened an account and placed all her money, nearly $100,000, in a checking account.

Then she was off to the university administration building. She had all her transcripts organized, and her correspondence from the Registrar's office at Florida Southern. She had written to them several weeks ago, just to

223

inquire about attending their school of medicine. They had invited her to come for an interview.

She walked up to the austere looking building and into the proper office. "My name is Suzanne Vasquez." She had decided to use her middle name. It was her way of declaring a new life for herself. After all these years, Caliente Suzanne Williams Vasquez was starting down a very long road toward fulfilling her dream of becoming a physician.

Chapter 49

Both men made only small talk as Frank negotiated the Interstate 25 traffic through Albuquerque. "This town has sure grown," Chui commented as they crossed over the stack of highways where Interstate 40 crossed. The car followed the green signs that pointed the way to Santa Fe.

"When were you here last?" Frank asked Chui as they finally headed north out of Albuquerque.

"It's been a long time ago. I came over here to do some recording. They have some great facilities here, believe it or not. Studio rates are a lot cheaper here because there is no union. We could fly over here and spend a couple of days recording and eat some good Mexican food and still save money."

"It looks like it might be a little wintry up in Santa Fe. Look at those clouds over the mountains."

"Good thing I brought my trusty old blue coat," Chui mused as they started up La Bajada Hill, toward the summit. From there one could see the entire city of Santa Fe.

"Yes. I see a little snow on the mountains up there. I know it is about the end of March, but it is still cold up here. It is always cold up here."

Frank passed the Cerrillos exit, drove on five more miles to the St. Francis exit. "I like this road. They named it after me!" Frank spoke out of the side of his mouth as though his joke was a secret. "Seriously, this is a shortcut to the plaza." Without thinking, and as he allowed a private thought to come out of his mouth, he said, "Your Grandmother Susie called me 'Francis' once. She said she didn't want to call me 'Father,' since I was much younger than she, so she called me 'Francis'."

"What are you talking about?"

Frank realized he was speaking of a time before Chui was born. "Oh, nothing, really. I was just rambling about the past. It was way before your time. I was just thinking out loud." That night on the beach kept haunting him. He swung onto his favorite little shortcut road, through the narrow streets of Santa Fe and past the unique "Merry Round House." That is what New Mexicans called their capitol building. Up ahead was the odd-shaped hotel, The Inn at Loreto. It shared a parking lot with La Fonda. He parked the car in a space toward the back and turned off the ignition. "Here we are. Leave your sax in the car for a while. We are a little early. I want you to meet someone first."

"Can we put it in the trunk?" Chui had ceased to be quite so paranoid about the treasure he had hidden in the bottom of his case, but he was still protective of it.

"Sure. We will be back in about half an hour."

The Inn at Loreto is a much newer hotel than the La Fonda. It was built in the 1980's. It was designed to look like the famous Taos Pueblo, with different levels. It was built around the centuries-old Loreto Chapel. Tourists by the thousands visit the Chapel each year to look at its stairway with no apparent support. The legend is that a poor wayfarer came to Santa Fe one day and entered the chapel. The sisters who operated the small building had a dilemma. They had a choir loft but no way to get to it. The stranger designed and built a stairway to the loft with no support. He took no payment. It stands today. Engineers and architects have studied the stairway and, allegedly, have not figured out why it works. Entry to the chapel can be gained either from the front door or from the hotel lobby. Frank led Chui into the hotel and toward the entrance to the chapel. A slim and very pretty Hispanic lady with long grey hair was standing there handing out brochures to the tourists as they entered the chapel. She had on a long, Indian print skirt and a turquoise concho belt. Her blouse was yellow with a very large turquoise bear claw necklace. She looked like a typical Santa Fe woman. Frank approached the lady from the rear and spoke to her. "I see you are doing your Sunday afternoon duty as usual." The lady whirled around and gave Frank a big hug and kissed him on the cheek.

"I wondered if you were coming today." She laid the brochures on a table and moved out of the doorway. "I can quit for the day. It's just volunteer anyway." Then she turned toward Chui. "Well, Chui, I guess you don't remember me? I am your Aunt Anna Maria."

Chui was dumbfounded. He thought he was having a dream. "I thought you were a ---"

Anna Maria finished his sentence "A nun? I was for many years. I gave it up. I am still a Catholic, but I realized I could serve much better in another capacity. It's a long story."

"Chui, your aunt has been a very important part of your life and you never knew it. Remember I told you I wanted you to meet some of my very special friends? Well, Anna Maria is among the most special. We have been friends for a very long time." He turned to Chui and said, "Let's go get your sax and play some jazz. Sister, you are coming over to the La Fonda, aren't you?" Father Frank had not become accustomed to calling Aunt Anna Maria anything but "Sister." He apologized and she laughed.

"You call me whatever you want. I even call myself that now and then. It has only been about five years, Father. Hey, I wouldn't miss it for anything. Let's go across the street. I want to hear my nephew blow some jazz on that sax."

Chui was struggling to remember the last time he had seen Anna Maria. It was a very long time ago. She was always somewhere down in Mexico at some mission or other. She always had on her black habit with the white stiff collar tight around her face. She looked so happy and free today. She almost skipped as she held tight to Frank's arm and walked down the street and across to the entrance of the old La Fonda Hotel. Chui picked up his sax from the trunk of Frank's car and was trailing the couple with the big case in his hand. He felt, somehow, so very happy for his aunt. He was happy for himself, too. He felt like he was walking on air. He seriously wondered if he had died and this was heaven. *"A couple of days ago, I was a homeless, hopeless, drunk, about to kill myself. What the hell happened? I don't really care what happened. I am just going to enjoy my life and hope I don't wake up in that awful doorway and this was all a wonderful dream."*

Chapter 50

It was not a dream. The hotel lounge was about half full of locals and tourists, waiting for the music to start. A hand-lettered sign stood outside the entrance to the lounge proclaiming "Jam Session Sunday at 2 PM."

Frank and Anna Maria entered the lounge and Chui followed close behind. Anna Maria found a table in the rear of the room and sat alone. Frank found some of his fellow musicians seated at another table and beckoned Chui to come over and meet them. A very large Navajo Indian man was standing with his arms folded. He had on a headband and a long ponytail hairdo. Chui half expected him to speak broken English and grunt. However, the big man stuck out his hand and grinned. 'You can call me 'Chief'. That's what everyone else calls me. I'm the drummer." Chui laughed at his erroneous thought. He supposed that some people expected him to speak broken English, too.

"I am pleased to meet you, Chief. I am Chui Vasquez. I play tenor. Frank invited me to play today."

The bass player said his name was Bill Sheets. He was called "Sheetsy." He ran a plumbing business in Santa Fe. There was a trombone player called Jack. He was a well-known disc jockey at a radio station in Albuquerque. The trumpet man was also from Albuquerque. His name was Charley. He managed a music store and played with the Albuquerque Symphony. Charley stuttered. It took him a long time to get out a whole sentence, so he didn't talk a lot. None of the musicians were "professionals." That is, they didn't play for their bread and butter.

The bandstand was a small stage in the corner. There was a piano and also an electronic organ. They were set up in an "L" form. Frank could position himself to play either the piano or the organ or both at the same time.

The motley group ambled onto the bandstand just before 2 o'clock. Each man had a drink in his hand. Both Frank and Chui got a glass of soda water with a slice of lime. It looked alcoholic but wasn't. Frequently patrons wish to buy the band a "drink." The bartender was told to bring Frank and Chui the soda water. It looked like a "drink" and satisfied the benefactor that he had done something nice for the musicians.

"Chui. You get to pick the first tune. You are the rooky today."

"How about something we all know well -- something to warm up with." Chui closed his eyes and thought for a few seconds. "Let's play 'Sweet

Georgia Brown.' A-Flat. Does that sound like a winner?"

"Let's do it." Frank pounded his foot and Chief picked up on the beat, clicking his sticks together. Frank laid down an eight-bar intro and the group was off and running. During the first two times through, each front man looked at Frank for instructions. Frank nodded at Chui and held up two fingers for the first solo chorus. Chief sent him off with his usual eight beat lead in as Chui closed his eyes and went into a wonderful trance. He could hear the other guys saying "nice" and "OK" and other encouraging words in the background as he played. It was a courtesy that musicians offer each other. The audience doesn't usually hear such complimentary words, but it is some of the food for the ego of the musician as he plays. It helps him play at his best. Chui finished his two choruses and Frank gave him the thumbs up. He turned it over to Jack. Chui opened his eyes and looked out into the audience. It had grown considerably and there was some polite applause for his work. He smiled and let his saxophone hang loose around his neck as he bowed slightly in response.

Jack played, then Charlie. Frank had turned in his seat and started to play the organ with his right hand. He let his left hand join in. The electronic organ had been stopped to play a "jazz" sound. Frank was fabulous. He hung his head over the keys and watched his own fingers fly over the keys. Chief shouted "Alright" as Frank hit a particularly nice chord. Chief was so large that he made the drum set look like a toy. But his touch was light and professional. He frequently shouted something complimentary and encouraging -- much like a teammate might shout to his fellow sports players at a basketball game. Chief was having a really good time this Sunday afternoon.

Chui wondered what happened to his aunt. He thought she must have joined some friends at a table around the corner from the bandstand. He was anxious to find out what Frank had meant about her influencing his life. He remembered that her father -- his grandfather -- Paco, had insisted that she remain a virgin. She was so beautiful and should have been allowed to have a relationship. She should have married and had children. But she was his only daughter and he was Hispanic. That combination frequently creates problems between father and daughter. He won. She went to San Antonio to a convent and became a nun.

Now she was apparently living in Santa Fe, flitting around a bar in the La Fonda Hotel. Old Paco was probably turning over in his grave. Chui laughed to himself. He couldn't help but feel a little vindictive against his stubborn old grandfather. Paco had ceased to acknowledge Chui after he ran off with that band all those years ago. Chui thought maybe he might have had some justification for his actions. He admitted that he was not exactly the perfect grandson. As a matter of fact, he was quite a renegade. He went off and left the aloe business in the lurch. But it didn't seem to have had much effect. The business thrived without him. Chui was having these thoughts while he was standing with his sax hanging from his neck, watching the crowd drinking and dancing all around him. He wished he had a drink. He had decided he had better not disappoint Frank, ever again. He must get that out of his mind. He would be happy with soda water and lime. Besides, it really didn't taste that bad.

After about an hour or so, Frank said he needed to pee and they all needed a break. Chui had put his sax case between the piano and the wall. He had not forgotten its valuable treasure tucked away. That package of hundred dollar bills had certainly changed his life. And he had not spent a penny of it. He still did not know whom it belonged to. He was having such a great time; he had nearly stopped thinking about it. He laid his sax on top of the piano and stepped down into the crowd. People he didn't know came up and told him how great he played. The break was short. He was glad. He came here to play, not to talk to strangers. He wondered what happened to his aunt. He didn't see her anywhere.

Chapter 51

By the time he was ready to leave his little winter home beneath the wing of his U-2, Major Johnny Vasquez did not know if it was 1963 or 1964. He thought maybe New Year's had passed by now. The winter days were very short here in the mountains of Finland and he was reluctant to leave. But, he knew it had to be done. He had all the survival gear he could carry. He had cooked and stored away his deer meat in the backpack he had fashioned out of the belts and upholstery in his plane. He had already made some snowshoes from some of the plane's wreckage. He needed to destroy the camera and equipment. That was his pledge to the CIA when he was assigned this mission. This was done expertly just as the sun came up over the eastern horizon. It wouldn't stay up long and he needed to get going.

It was surprising how well he negotiated the steep hills and trees in this barren, frozen land. He never was in any real danger of getting lost or of freezing to death. He had been trained in this sort of thing, but that was pretend and this was real. He had all the necessary equipment, a compass and warm clothing. The snow was not as deep as he thought and he made quite a nice distance down the mountain during the first day.

He had lots of time to think as he carefully picked his way down the mountain and across the valleys. He decided his first duty was to let someone know he was alive. He knew the Russians would say he had been shot down. It was not fair to let his family think he was either dead or a prisoner. He would find some civilization and get the word to someone. But who? Anna Maria, his sister. She would be the one who would handle it right.

As he trudged through the snow in Finland, his thoughts went back to Cali. It was so ironic that he had flown this last mission out of Laughlin in Del Rio. To keep the Russians guessing, the CIA insisted that the U-2's go on these missions from different bases throughout the world. He never knew exactly where he would be sent. This time, he was about ten miles from where he was born. He had some sort of intuition about this mission. That prompted him to write the letter to Cali and send it to Jim Williams by base mail and ask him to deliver it to his daughter but not to let her know any details. He put a short note in with the letter for Jim, but not to be read by Cali. He knew that Jim knew about his "problem" and probably had something to do with his reassignment. He was at Laughlin for only a few hours and seized this opportunity to get the letter, secretly, to his wife.

He had lots of time to formulate his plan as he managed to pick his way through a forest on a steep hillside. His next chore, he decided, would be to find Robin. He didn't know where he was but they both had their lives dramatically changed by the government and the Air Force. He hoped he was still alive and well. And he hoped that he was still available. He didn't know how he should deal with the government. As long as he was "missing," he could get all sorts of benefits. It was sort of nice to be "dead" but still alive. He recalled reading Mark Twain's adventures of Tom Sawyer, where they hid in the church and watched their own funeral after they were missing and thought to be dead. He laughed out loud at his prospects with this interesting combination. He continued walking hour after hour, getting ever so much closer to beginning his new life.

It was four days, or was it five days, into his adventure when he spotted some smoke in the distance. Although he had warm clothing, he had not been toasty warm for many days, he didn't know how many. The smoke was coming from a chimney down in a valley. He was suddenly in great need to warm himself by a fire. He picked up his speed as he trudged along through the snow. It was nearly dark again as the short day came to a close only about six hours after it started. The big farmhouse looked so inviting. It was like a Christmas card – a Currier and Ives. He could see the lights getting closer now. He walked up the lane to the front door and knocked. He could hear the latch being unlocked. A very large bearded man opened the door a crack and peered out at Johnny. "Ya," he spoke. Johnny did not understand Finnish, but he did know English and Spanish and had studied German.

"In his best German he said, "I am an American. I was lost in the mountains many days ago. May I enter your house?"

"Ya. Come in. You are velcome here."

That was the beginning of what was to be a month-long journey by horse and wagon and old farm trucks. He was fed and warmed and given shelter by some of the most wonderful, generous people he had ever met. His German and English were good enough to communicate. He explained that he needed to get to a phone where he could make a call to the United States.

He was into Sweden before he was able to find a city large enough to have international phone service. His first call was to the convent in San Antonio to find out where his sister was. He knew she was probably in Mexico, but where? They reluctantly gave him the information. The next step was to reach her by phone. After days of waiting, she finally returned his call. "Juanito. Is this really you? This is not a joke, is it?" The connection was intermittent but good enough.

"Yes. I am OK. You must NOT tell anyone that you have spoken to me. I need your help. You are the only person I have told that I am OK. I am in Sweden. I am going to Amsterdam, Holland. I will call you from there."

The two siblings exchanged sufficient information to schedule a contact from Amsterdam.

Next step – Find Robin Vanstreen.

In 1964, Amsterdam, Holland, was portrayed as the most liberal city in the world. Prostitution and drugs were legal. But, uppermost on Johnny's mind was its acceptance of what had come to be called "gays." He knew that he needed to find such a city to reunite himself with his friend and lover.

Anna Maria had contacted him and sworn herself to secrecy about his location. She had sent him money and told him she would come up with a plan to allow him to live his life under a new identity.

But his primary quest at this moment was to contact Robin. Anna Maria had told Chui that his father-in-law had retired to New Orleans and his mother-in-law had been diagnosed with Alzheimer's

He had trusted Jim once before and was about to do that again. His sister was able to get Jim's new address and John wrote to him seeking his help in finding Robin.

When Jim Williams received the letter from Amsterdam, he had no idea who would be writing him. He had a moment of elation as he glanced at the sender's name at the bottom. The letter was simple. *"Thank you for delivering my letter to Cali. I need another special favor from you. I think you are aware of my situation with the Air Force. My friend's name is Robin. Can you find out where I might contact him?"* He gave Jim his address. He purposely left out any last names -- just in case.

Jim was so happy that his son-in-law was alive and well, he immediately contacted John Bainbridge and began a few days of detective work to get Johnny the information he wanted. He did one more thing. He felt the need to call Johnny's mother and tell her he was still alive and well. He thought Johnny would approve. He would have contacted Cali, but he didn't know where she was.

In 1965, the CIA office in Houston was in a rather public building in the downtown area. It had taken Anna Maria many months to locate the proper person for what she had to say. It began in Washington and on to Los Angles and on and on through person after person. She was put on hold for probably enough time to fly around the world and back. She had spoken to evasive people. She had spoken to people she knew were lying to her. The persistent nun had learned how to determine who could help and who was "bullshitting" her, as she would put it. However, with all her determination and perseverance, she finally managed to find the right person.

Dallas King was the perfect stereotype for an old Texas Ranger who had become an agent for the FBI and was eventually transferred to the CIA in Houston. He had the exact dialect – a perfect match with Rex Allen. After all these months, Sister Maria had finally reached her contact. "We need to talk. But not on the phone. I can come to Houston. Can we meet?"

His deep voice had authority but was smooth and soothing. "You bet. When would y'all like to meet?"

The time and place was arranged and Sister Maria and her companion, Sister Delores, got aboard a bus and made their way from Laredo to Houston.

They met in a park. It was the spy novel meeting place for an informant and a CIA agent – but it worked well. "We travel in two's. Whatever I know, she knows." Sister Maria put him at ease with the presents of Delores. "I have a deal to offer the CIA."

Dallas was accustomed to talking to informants and all sorts of strange and interesting people, but this was his first deal with a couple of nuns. "I am listening."

"Let's say that a couple of nuns who have a legitimate mission in all sorts of small villages and towns in Mexico just might be able to pick up all sorts of information that might be of interest to the CIA. Let's say that these nuns might be able to document and verify this information. Let's say

241

that a couple of nuns would not be likely to cause any suspicion but might be taught whatever they need to elicit information from certain people and friends or families of people known to be suspicious and who might be a threat to the security of the United States."

"HOLD ON! You are going way too fast for this old Texan. So let's cut to the chase. Do I understand that you two are offering to work for the CIA as spies?"

"Well." Anna Maria was sobered by the sound of those words. But she knew that however sinister they might sound – the words were true. She paused for several seconds. "Yes. Yes, that is exactly what we are offering."

"Hmmm." Dallas rubbed his chin and pushed his big Stetson hat back off his forehead.

"There is a quid pro quo. We want you to know that going in. I guess you know what a quid pro quo is?"

"M'am. He looked her straight in the eye. "I may look and sound like a good ole Texas boy – and that I am – but I do have a law degree from SMU. I have heard the term once or twice."

Delores covered her mouth and giggled. Maria apologized. "Of course -- I am sorry. I just wanted you to understand that we have a rather strange but very serious request for our payment.

We do not want money. We want some files and records adjusted. Not deleted – just adjusted a little tiny bit." She held up her thumb and index finger to indicate how small her request would be.

"I have no idea what you are talking about."

"Well, I can't go into detail until we have a deal. We will work with you anywhere in Mexico that we can get into without suspicion. We probably have enough information, already, to earn our way, but we will work for five years undercover. But it must be *our* way, of course. We will continue to do the Lord's work and maintain our vows of the church. But we will agree to work for our government as CIA spies, as you so aptly put it."

"This is the damnedest offer I have ever had. You must know we have checked you two out thoroughly and probably know more about you than you do?"

"We figured you did."

"One of us has to trust the other, so I will start. OK? You got a deal. We need your help down there. Can you trust me to uphold my end of the bargain until we get the details worked out?"

The two nuns nodded in the affirmative.

"Now – what's the quid quo pro? What do you want?

"I want a certain CIA agent whose whereabouts is in question to be forgotten about. He has more than fulfilled his obligation, but he is ready to move on with his life. I want him to be free to go about his business without any fear of any repercussion or any future problems regardless of what might come up in his record. I want you to give him a new identity and forget all about him."

"What the hell did he do wrong – trash a U-2?"

Anna Maria sat stunned at his comment that appeared to be a joke. She decided to call his bluff. "Yep. That is exactly what he did. He trashed a U-2. And I want the CIA to forget all about it and pretend it never happened. And I want him to become permanently listed as 'killed in action'."

"Holy Jesus, I was joking, Sister. I think I know what you are talking about now." Dallas suddenly realized she was not joking and he remembered the incident very well. "But I guess for what you are willing to do for us; we can manage to do that little adjustment. You will be working directly with me and only me. We will need to set up a means of communicating so we can all stay safe and sound. I hope you pardon my candidness, but you two are far too pretty to get hurt. I am sure we will get to know each other quite well in the next five years. I hope so, anyway.

SO -- now that we have an agreement, I will be in touch. Y'all can just wander away now. I'll just make like a guy asking directions from a couple of sisters in the park. Sound like a plan?"

Chapter 52

Chui Vasquez was off in a wonderland in Santa Fe, New Mexico. On this same Sunday afternoon in Del Rio, Texas, his old grandmother was having a meeting with her attorneys. Aranda Vasquez had managed to survive a few scrapes with death over the years. But her good health and her good genes had given her nearly a century of life. She was 96 years of age now. Although she was frail, she still managed to walk and think on her own. Paco had died twenty years ago. He had a stroke. Her two eldest sons, the twins, had gone through two wars and had retired from the Marine Corps. They now lived at the Veteran's Home in Clearwater, Florida. Neither of them had married. Her daughter had been conned, by her father, into becoming a nun. Randa shuddered at this thought, not wanting to admit it. But it was too late not to deny the truth. Her husband had been in control of everyone in his sphere of influence until he died. Old Paco was a bit of a tyrant. He ran the show. If someone did not agree with him, he disowned them. He would disown his daughter right now if he were alive.

Paco had certainly been a good provider. He meant well and thought he was doing the right thing. But there was no room in his life for any disagreement. He died, believing his youngest son, Juanito, was killed as he flew a secret mission. He never knew why he had been assigned to this mission. He was missing in action and presumed dead. His wife had run off and had never come back. He disowned her, too. He presumed she was some sort of "Hippy" or other degenerate – no doubt on drugs, living in sin. But he had no idea what had really happened to her.

Paco was, however, a smart businessman. He had entered into an agreement with that big radio station in Mexico, to manufacture an aloe vera cream and sell it to the world. When the radio station was shut down for lack of maintenance, he seized the opportunity to market his cream elsewhere. His crop and cream had made a lot of money.

This was the subject of her meeting with her attorneys on this Sunday afternoon. They were meeting in the "spring house." This was her favorite place. It was originally a small building, enclosed in screen and open to the air. It had been remodeled some years ago. Today it is still a separate building, but it is enclosed and climate controlled. It has retractable windows and awnings. It can be open or not, depending on the orders of Randa. Today it is closed. But the atmosphere is the same. It looks out over the ranch, with beautiful landscaping all around. It is March and the cool weather has caused the flowers and trees to wilt. But the landscapers maintain the scenery quite well, defying Mother Nature as much as possible.

Randa is helped to the springhouse by her companion of ten years. "Dee Dee. What would I do without you?" Randa leans on her much younger friend as she walks through the breezeway and into the spring house. "Bobby and Ed will be here in a few minutes. Just bring them out when they get here." Roberto Garcia and Edwardo Gomez are the attorneys at the G and G Law Firm. They have been retained by Aranda Vasquez for several years. They were both graduates of Del Rio High School.

Randa sat down in her favorite chair, facing the huge lawn. She thought about her life. She had to take over the ranch after Paco died. Everyone thought she would fail – she was so shy and incapable. She smiled and nearly laughed out loud at that thought. *"I guess that notion didn't last for long."* There were several attempts to take over her lucrative ranch. There were several attempts to engage her in love affairs. *"I guess they thought I needed a man in my life. I can't say it wasn't tempting.* "She grinned at the thought.

Dee Dee sat down across from her on the couch. "You need anything?"

"Why don't you make some of your famous tea? You know -- the kind with a tiny little shot of brandy in it?" Her old eyes sparkled at the thought of a small amount of booze to warm her up a little. "You betcha, Mrs. V. I know just the way you like it."

She laid her head back, closed her eyes and thought about the call from Jim Williams. The words rang in her head even today, years later. "RANDA – I THINK JOHNNY IS STILL ALIVE." Those were the most precious words she had heard in her entire life. Jim went on to explain that it was top secret and she was not to mention it to anyone. During the conversation, he had told Randa his Susie had died a few months ago, of Alzheimer's disease. Randa expressed her sorrow at his loss. But she had seen Susie before they moved and she was failing, even back then. Jim explained that he could not promise anything, but he wanted her to know that Johnny was alive.

Randa asked him about Chui. He said he was afraid that Chui was lost somewhere in the world. He said he had seen him over the years, off and on, but finally lost track of him. He explained that he had become an alcoholic. *He stayed drunk most of the time he was here. We played some gigs here in New Orleans but he just disappeared one day. I will keep trying to find him.*

Randa was watching some squirrels playing in the yard as she thought about her conversation with Jim Williams those years ago. She didn't need to ask him about Caliente. She already knew what she was doing.

"Bob and Ed are here."

"Bring them in, Dee Dee. Bring them out here."

249

The two attorneys came through the springhouse door, entered and sat down on the couch across from Aranda Vasquez. "You want some tea?"

The two shook their heads, "No thanks." They spoke in unison.

"It's spiked up with a little brandy." Randa's eyes sparkled again at her better offer.

"Well, sure. That sounds like a nice Sunday afternoon toddy!"

"What is the latest offer?"

Ed spoke first. "They will pay ten million for the whole deal."

"Mrs. Vasquez. That is a lot of money!"

"I know. But this has been my baby since it was born. I can't give you a final answer just yet. Give me a little time. I know I haven't long on this planet, but I think I can last until I know what is the right thing to do. I just need a little more time. Go tell them I am considering their offer, but I am *not* going to give this business away. Aloe has now been discovered, and I helped build it. Anyway, let's enjoy our tea and talk about it in a few days." Randa's old hands were gesturing into the air as she spoke. She was obviously very possessive and emotional about her little aloe company and its products.

Dee Dee poured another small cup of tea for each man and for Randa. The three sat, sipped their tea and made small talk about the weather and the local politics and other mundane things. Finally the two lawyers got up and ask if there was anything else to talk about. As they were about to leave, Randa looked around as if someone might be listening and spoke quietly in a whisper. "Did you see to it that my mission was accomplished?"

The two men spoke as one. "Yes, Mrs. Vasquez, your mission was accomplished."

Chapter 53

The table that Aunt Anna Maria had claimed for the afternoon was difficult to see from the bandstand. It was around the corner in the big lounge. The hotel had been built long ago and was held up with big square pillars. This was a good engineering feat for keeping the building from falling down, but it was a pain in the ass for people who wanted to see the band perform. Anna Maria had chosen a table behind one of these pillars and was, therefore, difficult to see from the bandstand. She had not been at the table during the break. Chui assumed that she had found some friends and moved elsewhere. He tried to ask Frank about it, but Frank shrugged his shoulders and Chui promptly forgot all about it. He put his soul into his playing on this Sunday afternoon. His dream seemed to go on and on.

He wondered why he had allowed the alcohol to dominate his life for the last several years. El Paso was the lowest point in his life. He didn't even remember how he got there. He didn't know how long he had been there. He thought it must have been a couple of years at least. He managed to play a few gigs here and there. But there was always the booze. And, finally, he played on the corner for change so he could drink. And that is what he did until two days ago.

He was thinking about these things, as he stood waiting for his "turn" to play. Grandpa

252

Williams had died. He had gone on a real binge after that. He went from job to job. He was good enough to get a gig whenever he needed one. He could make good money. He had been in demand as a studio musician in California. But, good as he was, the studio could not allow him to come to work drunk. He thought he could play great – but only he thought that. It only seemed to be great. He was sloppy, he remembered, feeling ashamed about his actions. He would get into arguments with the studio bandleader as to how a certain song should be played. He might have been right, but it was not his place to question. And, all this came about because he was a drunk. Then, somehow, he got to El Paso and, after all these years, here he is on this nice day in Santa Fe, playing some jazz with some guys who love to play as much as he does.

All these thoughts were swirling around in his mind as he listened to his fellow musicians play their choruses on the bandstand at the La Fonda Hotel lounge on this Sunday afternoon.

They were playing "All the Things You Are" and it was his turn. He was a little apprehensive about this tune. It changed keys about a zillion times. He could have shook his head and passed on playing a solo, and the crowd would not have known the difference. But he decided to have a go at it. When a musician gets "lost," the piano man can lead him through the tune like a seeing eye dog to a blind man. As Chui played the difficult song, Frank began to hit the chords heavier than usual.

Chui remembered his grandfather would do that sometimes way back when. He managed to get through the song reasonably well, with Frank's help. He finished and turned to Frank. "Thanks, man. Thanks for the help." Frank winked at him and grinned. He was glad to help him out.

"Maybe we will practice that one a time or two before we play it again," he laughed. The other guys agreed. Chui felt like he had a family again. The day was about over. Chui did not want it to end.

Frank kicked off "Bill Bailey," which the group could play with their hands tied behind their backs, so to speak. Chui was swaying back and forth when he spied his aunt's yellow blouse way in the back of the room behind the post. He moved over to improve his view and saw that she was sitting with two lady friends. One lady seemed to be Oriental. The other had her back to Chui. They were having a glass of wine and talking. *"I sure hope she is having some kind of male relationship."* Chui realized his aunt's love life was none of his business. He closed his eyes, as usual, and played his two choruses of Bill Bailey with ease and perfection. The crowd clapped. They were louder and more boisterous now. He knew it must be the booze. He was thinking how alcohol could be such a nice relaxing, fun beverage. *"But not if you drink it like a fish."* The crowd clapped and he bowed in appreciation.

He turned to Frank. "What's next, Boss?"

Frank looked around as though he was checking out the audience. "You know, Chui. I would love to hear your rendition of 'Body and Soul' again. I haven't heard you play it since last Friday!" He laughed at their private joke. "You just take off and we will follow you. He grabbed the mike and told the audience that they were going to hear a special rendition of Body and Soul by the sax player. Chui was unprepared for this showcasing of this song. But he closed his eyes tightly, put the mouthpiece in his mouth, took a breath and began.

It was strange how he could get into this song. He played the first four bars all alone, as the crowd got quiet. Frank, Sheetsy and Chief came down very quietly with the bass and drums and eased in on the fifth bar, giving him a beautiful background. He could feel the hair stand up on his neck as he played on. He squeezed his eyes ever so tightly closed as he allowed his fingers to roam over the keys. He leaned over and then raised his instrument up and down with emotion. Jack and Charley filled in with some nice whole notes behind him as his saxophone sang away on the first sixteen bars. He had never played the song better. Frank's wonderful chords were perfect. They were quiet but firm, allowing Chui to improvise more than he had ever dreamed he could. The bridge went without hesitation. The sharps and flats slipped by exactly as Chui commanded. He was extending his notes to the very peripheries of the melody, without stepping over the line. Chief played a few bars in double time and Chui grabbed the double beat and allowed his improvisation to become even more difficult. The big drummer was moved to give his approval, nearly inaudibly. But Chui heard it and played even better. He simply could not make a mistake, regardless of how he pushed himself to deviate from the melody. He played the song twice through. He was the only one who played a solo, except for the background of the piano, drums and bass, and the wonderful chords played by the trombone and trumpet. It was his song, only his. He brought it to a close with an obbligato he had never tried before. It was played perfectly. He drew the last note out, not wanting to end the song. But it was time. The silence was deafening. The room was full of noisy people, who had stopped talking and were listening. He slowly opened his eyes. A beautiful older woman was standing right in front of him with tears running down her cheeks. Chui didn't understand what was going on. She was the one who had been sitting with his Aunt Anna Maria. The crowd was still silent. The woman looked up at him and finally spoke through her tears. "That was beautiful, Chui. I love you. I am so very, very proud of you." She grabbed him and hugged him tightly as she sobbed.

Chui didn't understand what was happening. He tried to be as polite as he could to this stranger who seemed to know him. He turned to Frank for an answer. "Chui, I told you I would have some surprises for you today. I would like you to meet a very special dear old friend of mine.

I have known this woman for many years. This is Doctor Suzanne Vasquez. Chui, this is your mother."

Chapter 54

"Dee Dee. Do you mind answering the phone for me?" Aranda Vasquez was still enjoying the warmth of the afternoon sun through the windows of the spring room. It was a little after 4 p.m. Delores brought the phone to her friend and handed her the receiver. "Yes, Sweetheart. How did everything go? (silence) I am so happy to hear that. (silence) Yes, Dee Dee and I have had a nice afternoon. We can hardly wait to see you. (silence) Yes, I know it might take a couple of days, but we will be here. We aren't going anyplace (laughter). Thank you for giving me a progress report. Call tomorrow and let me know how things are going, OK? We will see you in a couple of days. Love you, too. Bye"

"Everything OK, Mrs. Vasquez?"

"Yes, Dee Dee, everything is wonderful. And I wish you would call me 'Randa' like everyone else does. I don't care if you are a black woman who is pretending like she is my maid. You have a college degree and a seminary degree. You were a sister of the Dominican order. You were a friend and companion of my daughter for years and you are a member of my family."

"Well, Randa, you don't beat around the bush, do you?" The black woman put her arms around her friend and companion and hugged her like a mother.

"I don't have time to beat around the bush. Time is ever so precious to me now."

"You know, when Anna Maria and I were forced to make that terribly difficult decision to leave the order, I was so lost for a while. You have no idea just how much it has meant to me to have a family to go to." Delores Washington paused for a few seconds as she gathered her thoughts. "I had no family. My parents abandoned me when I was a baby. I was raised in a catholic children's home in San Antonio. I was devoutly religious. It is all I ever knew. So I went to the convent, like I was told to do. Then I met your Anna Maria. She was my salvation. We were soul mates. We were inseparable for years. We worked together. We lived together. We traveled together. We even 'spied' together. And when we finally had to make that terribly difficult decision to leave the order – we even did that together. Only thing is – she had a place to go and I didn't. So here I am."

"You make me cry when you tell that story."

"Well, you are stuck with me. I have adopted you as my family and now I can hardly wait for the next exciting chapter. It sounds like it is about to begin in a day or two."

"It certainly is, Dee Dee. It certainly is. Now, before we start slobbering all over ourselves, can you get me some of that wonderful tea you make so well?"

Chapter 55

All the emotions one could muster were catapulting through Chui's brain and soul. He wanted to say, "Where the hell have you been? Where did you go all those years? Why did you leave me? Why didn't you come back?" Question after unanswered question charged into his mind as his mother released her grasp on his shoulders. His saxophone was still anchored to his neck by the strap. He gently pushed her away a few inches, raised the neck strap over his head and placed his sax gently on the piano top. He turned and saw his mother for the first time since he was eleven. He looked at her and took in her wrinkled face and gray hair. She was still crying. He looked at Frank, who shrugged his shoulders and smiled away some tears. He stepped down the short step from the bandstand to the floor, put his hands on his mother's shoulders, formulated his words and spoke directly to her face. "I am fifty-five years old. I have been waiting for this moment since I was eleven. I prayed over and over that it would come before I died. I nearly gave up. Even through the depths of hell as a homeless bum and hopeless drunk, I held on and thought about you and Dad. And now through the good graces of this damn frigging priest who has befriended me for some strange reason, here you are. I don't know why and I don't know how. But someone has been helping me to this moment in my life. And I must tell you, Mother, I should be really pissed off, but this is one of the happiest moments of my miserable life." He grabbed his mother and nearly squeezed the life out of her.

Neither said a word for several minutes. The crowd seemed to sense that this was a private moment and treated it as such. Anna Maria finally approached and the two separated. "Your mother has a lot to tell you, Chui. And I am sure you have a lot to tell her, too."

Frank appeared, wiping the tears from his eyes. "How's that for a surprise, ole buddy?"

"You are a real shit, you know, you frigging priest. You could have told me."

"We didn't know for sure if she would make it. She is still a practicing Doc, you know."

"No, I don't know. But I can't wait to find out. What the hell is next?"

"Well, let's go outside and see." Doctor Vasquez looked at Chui like it was Christmas morning and he had gifts to open. "I think we might have a few more surprises." Chui plucked his sax from the piano top and put into his case. He quickly raised the little flap and poked his finger in to check on the envelope. It was there, but it didn't seem to matter much right now. He thought it might all be a dream. He snapped the case shut as he had so many thousands of times and checked to make sure it was secure. He picked it up in his right hand. Anna Maria and Father

Frank led the way. Cali snagged her son's left arm and held on as though he might run away. The four walked around the corner and across the street to the big parking lot of the big hotel and there before them was the biggest Motor Home Chui had even seen. On the side was written in huge letters "DR. V and the HEALTH MOBILE."

"We are going in style, Chui."

"Where the hell are we going? And, what about the car and my clothes and my blue coat?"

"Don't worry – I have that all handled. Just wait here until I go get my car." In a very few minutes, Frank drove his car up behind the big motor home – very close. He got out and opened the trunk of his car and asked Chui to come and help him. He retrieved a metal object that was a "V"-shaped frame. "You hold this up to the front of the car and let me put in the pins." The ends of the frame exactly matched two brackets that had been installed on Frank's car. The frame was inserted and the pins put in with Cotter keys and it was securely attached. The vortex was a "hitching" device that fit over a hitch ball on the motor home.

"What the hell is this?" Chui asked.

"It's a tow bar. Haven't you ever seen one?"

"No – can't say as I have. My life didn't include such things. What are we going to do with it?"

"It is used to pull a vehicle behind a motor home."

"Looks like you might have done this before," Chui noted rather suspiciously.

"Well – yes – a couple of times, I guess." Frank grinned and sounded a little guilty.

Chui held up the hitch of the tow bar until Frank expertly moved the car into place behind the big motor home. It was dropped onto the hitch ball and clamped down securely. He located a set of wires from under the car bumper and plugged it into the receptacle on the motor home. The safety chains were quickly attached to the hooks on the hitch designed for that purpose. "The lights are now connected to my car lights," Frank explained to Chui as though he were a child, just learning.

"Now what?"

"Get in. That's all there is to it. We are ready to go."

His mother and aunt were still standing just outside the door of the motor home, huddling together. The Santa Fe afternoon had begun to turn into evening and with it came a chill in the air. It was still March and not yet summer. Chui was too excited to be cold.

The door opened and they all started to enter. It was warm inside. The big vehicle had been running for a while. As Chui entered he saw, sitting in the driver's seat of the gigantic vehicle, the Oriental woman he had seen sitting with his aunt and the other lady while he was playing. Now it was clear to him. The other lady sitting at the table in the lounge was his mother. He allowed the two women to enter the motor home first. As Chui went in through the open door, he came nearly face to face with the most beautiful Chinese woman he had ever seen. She looked over at him and said, "No tickee, no seatee. Chop Chop. I givee you bes flont low. You be, how you say, co-pirot? I dlive dis biga bus. OK Big music man?"

Chui was confused by this Pigin English. He just nodded his head and said "OK. This front seat is fine by me. UH – Thank you."

" Dlive many time – many mile -- you don wolry – I vely good dliver." Chui was wondering what he had gotten into. He heard a little chuckle from the rear but paid little attention. Even though she was beautiful her English was terrible. He looked at her again and blinked his eyes a couple of times, wondering how he was going to have a conversation with someone who's English was definitely her second language. He was about to accept his fate. Then she, and the entire bus load exploded in laughter. "Hi, Chui. Have a seat. I'm

Vicky." She said in perfect American English. "Just a little joke to welcome you to our little family." She stuck out her delicate hand and smiled as she looked at him through her wire-rimmed octagonal eyeglasses. Her perfect white teeth shown between her sensuous red lips. That smile was so captivating. Chui was instantly smitten.

"You sure had me fooled. You did a good job with the Pigin English. Brought back a few memories when I was playing in San Francisco," he laughed.

He stuck his sax case behind the seat and turned around so he could look her over again. She had on a snug black skirt and red blouse. Chui could not help staring at her. She was the cutest, most beautiful woman he had ever seen. And he instantly loved her humor. She looked to be in her forties. English was so incongruous coming out of such a beautiful Chinese mouth – her Americanized English was actually perfect.

"Chui, this is my partner in crime. You will have to excuse her practical joke." His mother introduced them. "In addition to thinking she is ready for a stand-up gig in a Comedy Club, this is Doctor Vicky Chen. She has been working with me for a few years. She is one of the best physicians I have ever had the pleasure to work with. She keeps me in stitches, no pun intended. And, by the way, she's a damn good driver, too."

He was laughing at her joke, which made her even more cute and attractive. She finally winked at Chui and made him blush a little. "Now I promise I will be serious from now on. I heard your special song. You are fabulous. I want to hear you play some more real soon." Vicky sat down and slid behind the steering wheel of the motor home. She seemed so tiny to be in command of such a vehicle. "Oh, don't worry." She sensed his trepidation about her capabilities at driving the big bus. "I drive this big tank all the time. No joking this time. I do know what I am doing. We just came from the Navajo reservation. If I can drive over there, I can drive anyplace." She laughed and Chui melted. "You will sit there in the copilot's seat." The other two women and Frank had gone to the rear of the hospital-on-wheels and buckled themselves in. Vicky pressed on the accelerator and the big bus eased out of the parking lot and onto the street. They were on their way to El Paso. Chui secretly pinched his arm and thought to himself, *"I don't know what the hell I have done to deserve this day. I played the best I have ever played – I found my mother –I still have fifty thousand dollars in my sax case -- and now, I think I am in love. What the hell do you suppose is next!"*

Chapter 56

It's the same Sunday afternoon in Key West. Florida. Key West is at the end of a peninsula protruding about 200 miles out into the Caribbean Sea. Tourists are told that it is the southern most point of the United States. The same sign also tells everyone who reads it that it is "90 miles from Cuba."

Regardless of its location or its historical significance – it is a very popular tourist area. People flock to Mallory Square for the daily sunset. They enjoy the multi cultural activities and especially the restaurants. There are scores of restaurants for an area only four by six miles. New restaurants spring up almost weekly. You can get anything from Mickey Dees to overpriced snooty seaside venues.

On this particular Sunday afternoon, there are two old gents seated at one of Key West's old favorites – Sloppy Joe's. It is one of the oldest bars, allegedly the place Ernest Hemmingway hung out and, perhaps, wrote some of his best stuff as he sipped his gin at one of the open-air tables.

The two old guys are not sipping gin – but, instead, Heineken draft beer. They are also peeling and eating some fresh boiled shrimp. It is a typical, beautiful, Key West spring day and the sun is shining into Duval Street. They are

267

watching the tourists pass by. They joke about the beer they are drinking. They were both retired from the Heineken brewing company in Amsterdam. They were not involved in the brewing of the famous Holland beer--they were pilots. They flew company executives to various cities in the world in the company jet planes. They laugh as they sip their beer and allow that each little sip helps with their retirement pension. They were each rewarded quite well for their service to the company.

One of the men is nearly bald, with a fringe of grey hair around the edge of his head. He keeps it covered with a baseball cap with the Heineken logo on its brim. He has blue eyes and a light colored skin. The other has a full head of hair. It is curly and grey. His skin is dark and leathery. They have been in Key West for several months. They flew here from Amsterdam in their own plane. When they retired, the company was about to retire one of their older planes and they negotiated a deal and bought the small jet plane. It is hangered at the Key West Airport. Although they are well past commercial flying age, they still maintain their pilot's licenses and fly quite often. They are known to their new friends in the Key West community as Rob and John.

The third round of beer is making them more relaxed and they begin to talk about the past. "Do you suppose anyone will ever find that goddamn airplane?" Rob poses the question and they both laugh.

268

"You aren't going to ask me to tell that story again after all these years?"

"Well hell yes, I am. I was a better damn pilot than you were back at old Laughlin. If I was lost over Finland, I would have landed in a big cow pasture where I could take off again." Robin was chiding his partner as they finished their third beer. "I want to hear all the gory details – just one more time."

"Well, they sure as hell haven't found that U-2 yet, that I ever heard, and it's been up there for over forty years. Hell, I couldn't find it myself – even if I wanted to. I destroyed the good stuff. Some Finnish hiker probably found it and didn't know what it was." They both laughed, again. Then John got more serious. "I still don't know what made me decide to do what I did. I knew that if I went on one more spy mission I would be shot down and either die or be captured. I had already flown over a hundred missions. My number was up. But I had a lot more life to live." He looked up at the ceiling of Sloppy Joe's restaurant and watched a ceiling fan slowly revolve. "It's hard for anyone to understand – even you."

John relates the story, again, that only a handful of people know about. He recalls his landing on a remote mountain shelf in the mountains of Finland in the middle of the night on Christmas.

His spy plane came to a stop after plowing through that deep snowdrift. He was able to retrieve all his survival gear and use the plane's huge wing as a shelter for several days. He tells Rob about gathering wood and sticks and making a shelter -- using the big wing as a roof. His survival gear included warm clothes, a big knife, some matches and a hand ax. He also had his service revolver – which was not a revolver at all – but a 45-caliber pistol. He was able to build a fire by draining out some jet fuel. "That was my cozy little home for several days while I tried to figure out what to do next. I had to wait 'til I knew the weather was stable for several days. I killed a big reindeer and cooked him over the fire. He kept me alive. Bless his heart, I will never forget him. I hope it wasn't Rudolph!" They both laughed and another round of beer and some more shrimp.

"After I got my bearings, I finally got up the guts to leave my little cabin in the sky and start down the mountain. I took along Rudolph and my survival stuff and took off down the mountain into the wild blue yonder." They both sang the Air Force song, quite irreverently. "Off we go – into the wild blue yonder – flyin' high into the sky!" They toasted and laughed.

John related the story he had told Rob so many times. Rob loved to hear it again and again. He told Rob, again, how he came to a village and identified himself as an American and was taken in by some Finnish farmers. They directed him to the closest town where he might find some way to communicate with someone.

"The one person I knew I could trust was my sister. If I told her not to tell anyone, she would not tell anyone." He had contacted the local diocese and told them he needed to find her – it was urgent. They were a little reluctant, but finally gave him a phone number in Mexico. Rob nods and listens to the story he has heard so many times. He never tires of hearing it again.

"I can't believe you thought I had forgotten you." Rob feigned a serious look and touched his partner's hand. "I couldn't believe it when Jim Williams called me."

The two men were reunited at the Amsterdam Airport when Robin Vanstreen arrived in 1966. He had been flying corporate jets for General Motors in Detroit. "I didn't want to try the airlines. I was afraid they might begin to check into my background. My dad had worked for GM and I had a little head start there." He had been contacted by Jim Williams and was given the information about Johnny. "I can remember that day like it was yesterday." Robin was smiling as he adjusted his cap and patted John on the top of his gray hair.

The two had been reunited in Amsterdam, where they could live in peace as a gay couple. They went to the big brewery together and did a sales job on the transportation department. The company had been using commercial travel. The two pilots convinced them to buy a corporate jet and hire them as pilot and co-pilot. It wasn't long before the company had grown so much they needed another jet – then another – until they had a whole fleet. Rob and John were appointed to head up the fleet and flew millions of miles all over the world, delivering both corporate personnel and beer for Heineken's Brewery. Johnny used Rob's last name. He became John Vanstreen. They considered themselves a married couple. It was OK in Holland.

Chapter 57

Vicky Chen craned her neck to see in one rear view mirror, then the other as she expertly maneuvered the big motor home into the narrow Santa Fe Street and out toward St. Francis Drive. She checked to see that Frank's car was following properly. It was. They rolled onto I-25 south and headed toward Albuquerque. From the crest of La Bajada hill they began the long descent past the Cochiti Lake. The sun was setting to their right, over the west mesa. It would be an hour before they got to Albuquerque.

Chui's passenger seat swiveled completely in a circle. He could face the front or the rear or anywhere in between. He could visit with the passengers. He could see out the windshield. He could also face the driver, which he did several times. He caught himself staring at her a couple of times. She glanced in his direction and he turned away, but caught her smiling at him from the corner of his eye. "Were you born in China?" He asked her awkwardly.

"Well, my grandparents were. But some of the older members of my family were brought to California as 'coolies' to work on the railroad. But that was a long time ago. I was born in Seattle."

"What brought you to the Navajo reservation? Do you speak Navajo?"

Chui felt a little tongue-tied – like a high school kid on his first date.

"That is a really good question." She put Chui at ease. "Years ago my grandfather moved from Beijing to what was then called Formosa – we call it Taiwan now. Win Yen Tsao was his name. Anyway, he came to the United States as a member of the Chinese Embassy and worked in Washington for a while. Then he got his citizenship and eventually got a position with a small college in Indiana teaching Chinese. He had received his Doctorate in Ancient Chinese Linguistics. He discovered that much of our ancient language in China was carried over to North America and became a part of the Navajo language. I learned some of the basics from him. That gave me a kind of head start. But mostly I picked it up from the people I deal with over there. It is a very difficult language to learn because it was not a written language – until recently it was only spoken. After I received my MD, I moved to Albuquerque. I met your mom there and we started our service to the Navajo people. We go over there several days each month. I discovered that alcoholism is a huge problem over there. I am really interested in learning more about it."

Chui was fascinated with her conversation. He wanted to continue talking to her but her mention of alcoholism was getting a little too close to home for him right now. He thought he should swing around and talk to his mother and Frank but he wasn't quite ready yet to open that can of worms. He just wanted to enjoy all this newfound dream world. He felt like something was happening and everyone knew about it but him. But that was alright for now. He was just enjoying being close to a real woman for the first time in a long time. He would just take things slowly. Apparently his mother and aunt and the priest felt the same way. They just rode along making small talk. Finally his mother broke the silence.

"We need to stop in Albuquerque at BCMC," Cali shouted from the rear of the vehicle. Dr. Vasquez, Anna Maria and Frank were all sitting around a table, but were strapped in with seat belts. The table served as a desk to check in patients when it was a portable medical center. But all the medical equipment had been stowed away into cabinets, returning the motor home back to its original state for the time being. Except for the smell of medicine and alcohol, one would never know it was a moving hospital.

It had two bedrooms, two full bathrooms and a fully equipped kitchen. There were also various chairs and couches, which could double as beds. Two big "push outs" could be automatically moved to expand it when it was parked, giving it yet even more room. It had its own generator, with enough power to run anything it needed to run. It was completely self-contained. All it needed was water and fuel.

BCMC -- Bernalillo County Medical Center -- was the headquarters for Dr. Vasquez's treks

275

into the Navajo reservation. "We don't get paid very much for our work so at least the government can provide the fuel for this monster."

Vicky expertly pulled into the hospital grounds and through the gate into the maintenance area. The attendant came out, waved and shouted through the open driver's window. "Haven't seen you docs for a few days. How are ya? Guess ya want her filled up?"

"Yah, Toby. Fill er up, we got a long way to go."

"Good thing you don't have to pay for this stuff. The price just went up again". Vicky signed the clipboard handed to her by Toby and waved goodbye. They traversed the hospital parking lot with Frank's car in tow and headed for I-25 again and toward Las Cruces and then back toward El Paso.

The sound of the silence in the big motor home was deafening to Chui. He knew someone had to start asking questions, and he had more questions then anyone else. It seemed to him that everyone in the motor home knew everything except him. He wasn't sure he wanted to open the can of worms. He was quite contented with the present right now. He wasn't sure he wanted to delve into the past, but knew he must do just that eventually. He was enjoying the closeness of Vicky. She smelled so good. He had not allowed himself to smell a woman's perfume for a long time.

He watched the sun finally disappear out his window, over the mesa, as they crossed to the west side of the Rio Grande River just south of Albuquerque. "Everything OK up there?" Frank's voice startled him as he broke the silence.

"It was until you woke me up." Chui tried to lend a little humor.

"Chui. Why don't you trade places with Anna Maria for a while?"

It was just the invitation he was waiting for but dreading. He turned toward Vicky and she could feel his reluctance to leave his seat. "I'm not going anywhere, Chui. You can come back in awhile."

He was embarrassed that she detected his emotions. But it also gave him a nice warm feeling about her. *"Maybe she likes me,"* he felt like a high school kid again.

"Yes, I think that might be a good idea. Let's do that."

The two passengers rose and traded places in the big RV as it moved along the highway at 65 miles per hour.

Chui sat down in a comfortable lounge chair close to the table where his mother and Frank were seated. "I sure wish you would get rid of that red shirt." Chui tried to inject a little levity into the situation. Everyone laughed. It did take away some of the seriousness of the moment.

"What do you want to know first?" His mother was the first to approach the subject of his past.

"I think I would like to know where my dad is." This seemed to be an unexpected first question but his mother took a deep breath and began to explain.

"Your dad is very much alive. He was sent on a very important and heroic mission many years ago. Do you remember reading about Gary Powers?"

"Sure. He was a U-2 pilot over Russia and got shot down and captured. What does that have to do with my father?"

"Your dad was also a U-2 pilot over Russia. He was nearly shot down with a Russian missile and he chose to land his plane on a mountaintop and walk away. He made it safely to Amsterdam, Holland. The CIA agreed to consider him as killed in action and give him a new identity."

"Why did they do that?"

Because your aunt Anna Maria and her companion, Sister Delores, agreed to become spies for the CIA while they were nuns in Mexico. That is why they are no longer sisters of the order. It's a long story. It was a choice they made to give your dad a free life to live as he wished."

Chui looked toward the front of the motor home as his aunt twisted around and faced him. "It is what family does, Chui. I would do it again in a heartbeat."

"Where is my dad now?" Chui was almost afraid to ask.

"This is the hard part, Chui. But I want you to know the truth, so here goes. I am not going to pull any punches. Your dad is a gay man and has been since he was born. He tried to be straight for years, but it just didn't work. He was discovered having an affair with another pilot and sent on this CIA mission as an alternative to being kicked out of the Air Force. Your Grandfather –my dad -- was extremely influential in this decision. Otherwise he would have been asked to resign, as his partner was. He was able to call your Aunt, Anna Maria and she and Dad helped him find his partner. He lived with his partner in Amsterdam. They were corporate pilots for many years and are now retired." Cali rushed through the history of Chui's father as though she needed to get it said in a hurry. Chui was quiet. He said nothing for several minutes.

The next question unexpectedly came out of his mouth. He didn't mean to be so blunt. But it was time to get down to the nitty gritty. "Is that why you ran off?"

"That is a fair question and should have been answered years ago, Chui." His mother was gentle and soft spoken. Not like he remembered her. "I knew from the time I was forced to go to Del Rio, when I was a teen ager, I was being a terribly spoiled brat who wanted to be given everything she asked for and if I didn't get my way, I had a tantrum. I was trying to punish my parents for disrupting my life. I was irresponsible and selfish. When I got pregnant with you, I tried to change and be civil and go along with whatever I was asked to do. I really tried, I really did. But I wanted in the worst way to be a doctor. I studied correspondence courses and realized that I had what it takes, at least academically, to do just that –be a doctor. I knew your dad was gay. I knew we would have no life together. I thought he was a prisoner of war, or worse. I had only one close friend in my life. Then he disappeared."

"Who was that?"

Frank spoke up. "You are looking at him, Chui. It was I. I let her down. I let everyone down. I was the most selfish of anyone. I let everyone down big time. Your mom – my church – my parish -- everyone."

"Well, not me, you didn't," Chui interrupted and directed this comment to Father Frank. "But how the hell did you find me last Friday?"

"I didn't find you."

"Then who did?"

"Remember your buddy at Motel 6? Remember ole Punj?" Chui's mouth flew open, but before he could speak, Frank continued. "Punj and I met at an AA meeting. He was a Hindu who became an alcoholic and I was a priest who became a drunk. We became friends. He fell off the wagon one night and I came to his aid. During his recovery, we talked for hours about our lives. He asked if he could come to my church and I encouraged that. As time went on, he learned of my heartaches in life. He learned that I had let your mother down and, consequently her son. I told him that one of the things I wanted to accomplish in my life before I went to my reward was to find my dear friend's alcoholic son." Chui was moved by Frank's remark. "But I had no idea you were right in my back yard. I didn't really look for you. I just talked about it to Punj."

"How long did this go on?" Chui was leaning forward in his chair.

"Well, I got to El Paso years ago. I guess I have been looking for you since your mother told me you were an alcoholic. Punj kept telling me about a homeless guy who played a sax on the corner a few blocks from his hotel. I didn't pay attention. I couldn't believe that it could possibly be you. Too much coincidence. I thought you would be down and out – but not THAT down and out. He finally convinced me to take a look. That took awhile. I kept putting it off. You weren't there every day, you know."

"I guess when I got enough money to get me a supply of booze, I took a vacation." Chui chuckled as he tried to remember.

"Well, anyway, I couldn't believe it but I finally appeased my friend, Punj, and went over there to your corner. We still weren't sure. It had been a long time. You were only eleven when I last saw you. I watched you for a few weeks, off and on. Then last Friday, I asked you to play. When I heard you do 'Body and Soul,' I just knew it must be you. Punj went over and put some extra money and his card in your case and you took the bait. You came to the motel. We were not a hundred percent sure it was you until you wrote your name on the hotel register. Punj called me and I called your mother immediately and you cooperated beautifully."

"So -- you and my mother have been friendly for quite a while?"

"A long while, Chui, a long while. She has been up in Albuquerque for a few years." Frank put his hand on top of Cali's hand and patted her lovingly. "That is why I knew the way to Santa Fe

so well. Hey, that would make a good song."
Frank did a little Diane Warwick parody: *'Do You
Know the Way to Santa Fe.'* Everyone laughed. It
broke the soberness of the conversation. It needed
to be broken.

Chui spoke next. "Do I get the idea that
there is more to your friendship than just
friendship?"

Frank looked at Cali and grinned and
winked. "Remember I told you I was sent to Santa
Fe to dry out? Well, one day after I got out of that
prison they called a home for alcoholic priests – I
went to play where we played today. I knew if I
could play in a bar, I could leave the booze alone. I
had cured myself. I went to the bishop and asked
to be reinstated by the Catholic Church and he
told me no. He refused my offer and told me to go
back to the prison."

"You already told me all that," Chui
reminded him.

"I know, but I left out a little part." Chui sat
up in his chair. Frank's spanish eyes sparkled a
little in anticipation of divulging a little tidbit that
Chui had not yet been told. "I told you I went to
El Paso because I heard of a Bishop there who was
more lenient."

"I remember you said he gave you back your
authority as a catholic priest"

"No, I did NOT say that. I said as a *priest.* Not a *catholic* priest."

"What are you trying to tell me, you friggin' priest. Are you a priest or are you not a priest? What is going on here?"

"You see, Son, I am now, and have been for years, an *Anglican* priest. I am an Episcopalian priest! I can choose to be celibate or not. I can choose to marry or not. The Catholic Church wouldn't take me back but the Episcopalians took me. And I have had a wonderful life ever since."

"Now hold on here. You mean you and my mother ---"

Cali interrupted and took up the story from there. "I worked in Florida for many years after I finished medical training. I got an offer to move to New Mexico and do some work on the Navajo Indian reservation. Vicky and I work with alcoholics up there. One day we decided to take a break and went up to Santa Fe on a Sunday afternoon. I walked into the La Fonda and heard this piano and organ playing in the bar. There was no band, just a piano player all by himself. We walked in and ordered a glass of wine and listened to the music. We didn't pay much attention to the musician until a 'local Santa Fean' at the next table leaned over and said, 'Betcha don't know what that piano player does for a living?' We thought it was a joke. I said 'plays the piano, I guess.' He said '*wrong*.' He is a priest!" My heart

284

stopped. I jumped up from the table. Vicky thought I had lost my mind. I ran up to the piano and looked. It couldn't be, I thought. I looked again and, mentally, put a white beard and moustache on Father Francisco and there he was."

Frank now took over the story. "She yelled at me -- 'FATHER FRANCISCO.' I about jumped off my piano bench. No one had called me that for years. I was Father Frank now. She came right up on the stand and grabbed me around the neck and sat down right on my lap and gave me the best hug I have ever had."

Chui was smiling and the rest of the RV passengers were laughing, including Vicky. "I thought she had lost her mind – hugging a perfect stranger in a bar in Santa Fe!" Vicky was shouting from the driver's seat.

"You drivee bus -- I tellee story," Cali shouted back in Pigin to her partner. Everyone roared with laughter.

"So, now what?" Chui asked the next question. "Are you – I mean since you are not a real priest – Well, I mean a real priest like I grew up with –" His words were coming all wrong.

"Are we lovers?" Frank paused briefly. "Yes, we are. Is that OK with you?"

"Well, hell yes, you friggin' priest. Hell, yes it's OK. I think it is great. But what about – uh – well -- dad?"

"Johnny has his life and -- thanks to your aunt – is able to live it privately with his lover. Isn't that the way it should be?"

"You bet it should. I'm an agnostic – I don't have any problems."

"I don't want to hear that." Anna Maria finally was moved to join the conversation. "I am still a Catholic, you know." She then laughed and so did Chui. "You *don't* go to your church and I'll go to mine."

"I have one more question. Were you at Grandpa's funeral in New Orleans?" Cali was relieved that Chui remembered her.

"Yes. Yes I was, Chui. I was standing off in the distance. It was your day to grieve for Daddy. I grieved, too, but it was your day. He was your soul mate, not mine. We had not really been -- uh – we just never were close after I..." She paused and groped for words. "I had to get back to the hospital. I had duties – patients – babies to deliver. I went to the house after the funeral and you were passed out. I am sorry, but that is the way it was back then. I had to leave. I thought it was better that way. I should have stayed but I didn't. I am sorry."

"That's OK, Mom, that's OK." She smiled and the matter was not brought up again.

"I think we have had enough serious conversation." Frank rose up and went to a closet and retrieved an electronic piano and sat it up on the table. He plugged it in to the wall socket, which was being operated by the generator. He cracked his knuckles a couple of times and said, "Chui, will you join me?" Chui couldn't wait to be asked. He grabbed his sax case and retrieved his golden tenor and put in the neck and mouthpiece. The envelope with the money didn't even enter his mind.

Frank began to play and sing – *"If you ever plan to motor west take my way -- the high way that's the best -- get your kicks on route sixty- six."* Chui stood in front of him and joined in the old Nat King Cole song. Frank did his best imitation of Nat singing the song. Cali wiped a tear from her eyes as she remembered that night on South Padre Island when she first heard Frank play and sing that song. Chui had no idea what she was thinking.

She was thrust back to 1950 at the Jetties Restaurant on a rainy afternoon. She had such a crush on the young priest. She thought she was in love with Johnny. But she had met Father Francisco at the school when he came to talk to the senior class about the Padre Island Trip. She was a rebellious teenager and thought this was a perfect opportunity to get herself into trouble and punish her parents at the same time. She began to flirt with the priest, knowing full well he was not, nor would he ever be, available. He was such "forbidden fruit." That is what made it so much fun. She could make Johnny jealous and piss off her parents and do something naughty all at the same time. She was young and immature and had no idea what she was getting into.

Then her mother came along and spoiled her fun. She could see her mother getting too friendly with the priest and took it upon herself to put a stop to that. When she saw her mother and Father Francisco staggering toward the cabana that night on Padre Island, she grabbed Johnny, pulled a blanket over them and took off her swimsuit top. She was ready to get into big trouble. That is when Father Francisco suddenly appeared and pulled them apart. *"I was so terrible,"* she was smiling now and seemed to be listening to the music as the big RV rocked down I-25, but her mind was a million miles away.

They passed Socorro. Frank and Chui kept on playing music until they approached El Paso. Anna Maria was anxious to get to where they were going. Vicky was patting her left foot to the music. She was enjoying it – but wishing she had her old copilot back. Something was going on with her heart that, even as a doctor, she couldn't explain.

It was about ten in the evening when they pulled into the Motel 6 parking lot. "We are going to stay here for a while?" Vicky was shouting back at Cali.

"Yes, Punj is expecting us. He would be devastated if we didn't stop and see him." Frank answered her question.

Punj came running out toward the RV and gave Vicky instructions as to where to park the big bus. He had a very large parking lot, capable of parking big semi trucks. They parked away from the rooms so they could run the generator without disturbing the customers. Chui was the first to jump out of the RV and run toward Punj. He gave him a big, unexpected hug. "What's that for? Hindus don't get that emotional. It's against our beliefs."

"I don't care right now. I think you know what that hug is for. You have been a very important part of my recent life. If it weren't for you, I would be sleeping in that doorway tonight and playing on that corner tomorrow —or I'd be dead. They told me the story. And, besides, hugging friends is the American way!"

"Well, it was the best I could do for my dear friend, the priest."

"Episcopalian Priest, I might add," Chui corrected him.

"Let's all go over to Denny's for some supper. I am buying." Punj was waving his hands around like a windmill. "Then you can all go to sleep in your motor home in my parking lot. No charge. I am almost full tonight, anyway."

****

With the touch of a couple of buttons on the control panel, the gigantic motor home expanded itself with two separate "push outs." This nearly doubled the size of the lounge area just behind the driver's seat. Chui was directed to sleep on the futon in this part of the home on wheels.

It was sometime after midnight when he sat up in his bed like a Jack-in-the-Box. He was soaking wet with sweat and having a terrible dream which he could not remember. His heart was racing and he could feel his pulse in his chest and his head. *"I need a drink."* This was his first thought. His second thought was that he was having a heart attack or a stroke. He felt tingling pricks, like a Texas cactus, sticking into his skin. He thought he could see bugs crawling on his arm and he scratched at them as he sat upright. He had no pajamas, so he was wearing his clothes and they were soaked. He didn't want to disturb anyone, but he was scared. Finally, in desperation, he called out into the dark motor home. "Help me, please. Someone help me!"

First on the scene was Frank, followed close by his mother and then Vicky. He did not realize it at the time, but he had two fine physicians as his beck and call. But this was of not much help at this moment. He was shaking violently and freezing cold. He was wet with sweat and scared and did not know what was happening to him.

"Hand me the BP cuff and let's get his pulse." It was his mother who was giving the directions as she removed his perspiration-laden shirt.

"180 over 100 at 136." Dr. Chen was reading the BP and pulse rate.

"That's a little high and fast but I think he'll be OK now." She had a quick listen to his heart with her Stethascope.

"Chui, how do you feel?"

"I'm freezing to death. Am I dying? Am I having a heart attack?"

"No, Sweetheart, you are having a reaction to the lack of alcohol." The doctor was suddenly his mother. "Just lie back down and we will take care of you 'til you get through this." She scooted over onto the futon and he laid his head on her shoulder. Vicky pulled a chair up and held his hand. She pulled the cover around his bare chest and arms. Chui immediately felt a feeling he had not felt for many years. He felt warm and loved.

"Damn, you can't beat this kind of care!" Frank squatted down in front of Chui so he could talk to him close up. "I wondered if you were going to get something like this, ole buddy. Most of us have been through it a few times. You are in the best of hands. We gotcha covered. Just relax and it will go away." Frank's voice was soft and reassuring. "I'll bet you are thinking 'if I just had a drink, it would go away. Right? Well, you would be right, it would all go away. But that's not this Doc's prescription."

Cali's right arm was around her son's shoulders, holding him while she whispered to her partner to get him a sedative to help him calm down. Vicky opened the padlocked chest in the back of the big hospital on wheels and retrieved a small hypodermic needle and filled it with a mild sedative. She gently and with little pain, injected it into Chui's right arm. "That will help get you through this," she told him as she patted him on the head. His mother kissed him on the forehead and laid him back down and covered him up. She took his arm and checked his pulse from the wrist. "He'll be fine now. Just a little case of the DT's. He'll sleep now 'til morning."

A gentle knock on the door was answered by Frank. It was Punj, who had seen the lights from his motel. "Everything OK here?"

"I think so, just a little withdrawal. We've all been through it, haven't we, my friend?"

"Yes, we have. But it doesn't make it any easier for the new drunks." Punj gave Frank a little gentlemanly hug as one fraternity brother might hug another. He went back to his motel.

Cali kissed her son on the forehead once more like he was only eleven years old. Vicky squeezed his hand before returning to their beds. Chui smiled and gently drifted back to sleep. Frank couldn't sleep for a while. It brought back some unforgettable memories.

Chapter 58

The west coast of Florida is a hot bed of retirees from all over the country. The sandy beaches are littered with expensive condos, stacked up in tall buildings with an ocean view. But all retirees do not live in such gargantuan structures. Strewn along the intercoastal waterway, near Clearwater, are some modest homes. Their lawns come down to the edge of the waterway and sport piers and boats of all sizes and price ranges. One such home was bought several years ago by a retired government worker. He moved to Florida from Texas when he retired from the CIA. His wife died of cancer five years ago. He has a forty-foot fishing boat and loves to take his friends out into the Gulf of Mexico for a day's relaxation. He misses his wife. But he has stayed in touch with a couple of old friends with whom he worked several years ago. His friends were both Catholic nuns. These sisters did secret work for their country that is still classified to this day. They became fast and devoted friends. They helped him through the death of his wife. Although he was a member of the Baptist Church, these two catholic nuns helped him more than he could express. He recalls what good work they did for the CIA and the United States Government. Few people will ever know what a contribution they made. They made it possible to get hundreds of drug dealers and potential terrorists off the streets. It was dangerous work. And they got little credit for it. Eventually, to maintain their top secret identity and the decorum of the order to which they were initiated, they left the order. They were forced to leave Dominican Order. It had to be that way. They could no longer be nuns in the church.

On this March morning his phone rang as he was finishing his second cup of coffee on his screened-in porch. It was one of those nuns. "Dallas? This is Sister Delores in Del Rio."

"My God. How y'all doin', Darlin'? How's your partner? I haven't heard from her for a few months."

"That's why I am calling. I sure don't want to poke my nose in where it doesn't belong and I know it is none of my business. But it sort of *is* my business. What I am trying to say is ---"

"HOLD ON. HOLD ON. You are confusin' this old Texan. But I think I know what y'all are tryin' to say. Are you trying to be a matchmaker again?"

"Dallas. She talks about you all the time. And you know we left the order years ago. I have known Anna Maria since we were kids. I mean, I know she – well – she just has never had a male friend."

"Jesus, Dee Dee. What are you trying to say? Spit it out, girl. Spit it out!"

"Well, we are having a kind of reunion here at the ranch house and I would like for you to

295

come over and surprise Anna Maria. I know she wants to see you again. And I think you would love to see her, too. Wouldn't you?"

"Well now. You are a little devil, aren't you? Of course I would. I miss her a lot. I think about her all the time. I just didn't want to push myself off on her. I didn't know if she was ready for that kinda thing or not."

"Well, someone has to take the first step. Tell you what. Can you be at the Clearwater airport this afternoon about one o'clock?"

"Damn. You don't mess around, do ya? I guess I can. I ain't doin' anything else today. Just watching the sea gulls. Can I take a shower first?"

"I need to make some arrangements. I'll call you back in a little while. You get ready. I am so happy. I am so happy. I just knew you would want to come.

****

The Clearwater, Florida, airport has become a very popular place for private aircraft to come and go. It serves the central Florida area without the need to fly into the gigantic Tampa Airport. A small waiting room serves the "general aviation" section. Seated in the waiting room are two old guys who have been told they would be taken for a nice airplane trip on this day in March. They attract some attention, because they are elderly. They no longer stand as tall and strong as they once did. They are, however, in superb health for their ages. But they attract attention for another reason. They are identical twins. They are Ramon and Damon Vasquez. They live in a veteran's home at the VA Hospital grounds in Clearwater. They live there because their entire lives have been devoted to the service of their country as members of the Marine Corps. They are waiting for their little brother to pick them up in a little jet plane with a Heineken beer can painted on its side.

Another tall man is seated in the waiting room also. He has on western boots and a big Stetson hat that makes him look even taller. He is pacing around watching for the same little jet with the Heineken beer can. It finally lands and taxies up to the walkway. The three are greeted by a bald man with a baseball cap and blue eyes. "Dallas? Ramon? Damon?" The three rise and identify themselves. "Your taxi is here." Robin Vanstreen shakes each hand. Behind him comes a small gray-haired Mexican man in his flight suit with the Heineken beer can on a patch above his left pocket. When he enters the door, the twins jump up together like they have been shot at.

"Juanito!" They shout together. Johnny Vanstreen holds out his arms and grabs his brothers and hugs them tightly. "We thought you were killed in action." What happened to you? Someone called and told us to be here. We couldn't believe it! We don't know what is going on."

"It's a very long story. I'll tell you all about it later." He turns to the Texan. "You must be my savior. Dallas King?"

"Well, hell yes. You must be the little Mexican with the bravest sister in the world. Hot damn, I am glad to meet you. And these gotta be your brave brothers. What a family. What a family. And y'all must be Rob. You are a pretty important part of this drama, too, you know?" He gives each man a polite hug and affectionate pat on the back.

Rob beckons to them. "Yes sir. I am so happy to meet all of you. Let's get going. Your private jet is waiting. Hope you like Heineken beer. That's all we serve on this jet." They all laugh and walk out to the little corporate jet and climb aboard.

Johnny is the pilot and Rob is the co-pilot. They get their clearance from the tower. It is just after two in the afternoon. They take off like a streak and pull nearly straight up. The little jet with the beer can painted on its fuselage climbs out over the beautiful Gulf of Mexico and sets the heading for the Del Rio, Texas, International Airport.

Chapter 59

Punj offered a couple of his nicer rooms to the group for their morning bathroom needs. The motor home was perfectly capable of accommodating them – but it was more convenient to use a normal bathroom. It was about 6 a.m. and the sun was just cracking over the eastern horizon of West Texas. Chui was the first to jump up from his futon and grab some of his clothes and head for the motel room and a hot shower. He had hoped the night time experience was a bad dream, but he knew it wasn't. He showered and dressed and returned to the motor home just as everyone was clamoring around, getting ready for the day. He tried to say something to his mother but she hugged him and put her finger over his mouth, as if to shush him. She whispered in his ear. "Chui, we all love you. We know you are going to be fine. Don't be embarrassed. Dr. Chen and I have seen this hundreds of times. It's part of your healing process. Let's just go on from here and if it happens again, we will be there again. Now, are we all clear on that?" Frank walked past him and patted him on the back. Anna Maria slept through the incident. Vicky just smiled and Chui melted again.

Punj was up and about. When he approached Chui in the parking lot, he ran his hand through Chui's curly hair and messed it up, then he winked at him. Chui knew why. Punj was sad to see everyone leave but knew it had to be. Everyone thanked him for his hospitality and the dinner at Denny's. They all needed to get on the road. Frank pressed the buttons that rolled the big push outs back to their travel mode. Coffee was brewing in the RV's kitchen. Someone had located some stale donuts in the cupboard. Breakfast would need to wait for a while. El Paso was bustling as they finally rolled onto Interstate 10. Cali decided to drive the bus for the first shift, giving Vicky a break. She sat on the couch next to Chui where he had spent the night, and had that frightening experience. She seemed to like that arrangement and so did Chui.

"Could I ask another question?" Chui shouted up to his mother. Frank was sitting in the passenger seat. Frank spun around and told him to shoot. "WHERE THE HELL ARE WE GOING?" Everyone laughed. They all realized that everyone knew what was happening except Chui. They had not bothered to tell him, yet.

Anna Maria was seated at the table across from Chui and Vicky, drinking her coffee, watching the West Texas countryside flash by. "We are going to a kind of reunion, Chui. Your grandma, Abuela Randa, wants us all to come and visit her. She has some things she needs to do and wants us all there. Now that we have found you, it is the perfect time."

"Isn't she getting pretty old by now?"

"She is ninety-six. But she is spry and sharp as a tack. She has been running the ranch since Dad died, but, even more than that, she has made the aloe vera business a huge success. She supplies companies all over the world." Anna Maria paused and took a big sip of her coffee and a bite of a donut. She talked with her mouth half full. "But she just wants to see her family while she is still alive. Daddy was such a powerful influence in the family. Bless his heart; he thought he was doing the right thing. But he was so demanding and --"

"He was a damn control freak!" Chui couldn't help letting that comment slip out of his mouth. Anna Maria stopped chewing and ignored it.

The big bus slipped its way down the road. Frank's car rolled along behind, nearly unnoticed. Cali announced that Van Horn was coming up. They were about two hours into the trip. That would end their interstate driving. It would be Highway 90 for the rest of the way to Del Rio. She pulled over into the parking lot of a big Texas restaurant and they all piled out for a big Texas breakfast.

After they returned to the RV, Vicky slid into the driver's seat. Chui quickly grabbed the passenger seat next to her. Not that anyone else wanted it. But he wanted to be close to Vicky and she seemed to want that, too. There were about five hours to go. They should be there about noon.

Chui was getting excited about seeing his grandmother. It had been years since he had seen her. He was ashamed of himself, but he always managed to find an excuse. He would always need to have one more drink and blot it out of his mind. After last night's experience, he thought he was a lot closer to getting rid of this demon than he ever had been. The droning and rocking of the motor home nearly lulled him to sleep. In his half awake state, he was wondering. He wondered why so many people had come to his aid. He wondered why he was here, in this place today, riding in a quarter million dollar motor home on his way back to his old hometown. He wondered who the hell gave him all that money that was still tucked away in his sax case -- and why.

****

He suddenly realized that Vicky was humming. She was unconsciously humming a song. It was "Body and Soul." She was doing pretty well with it, he thought. She even managed to stay on key. He looked at her and watched her hands grip the wheel. He wondered how many lives those little hands must have saved or cured or took away the pain. He looked at her legs. She had put on what looked to be a short, blue skirt that was really a pair of shorts. Her white silk blouse matched perfectly. She looked so sexy. He shook off the thought that was about to drive him crazy. "Nice tune," he said.

She spun her head toward him and looked embarrassed. "I didn't know you were listening." She smiled that smile that Chui had come to understand would melt him away like a piece of ice in the hot Texas sun. "I am not much of a singer, but I did study music a little. I play the guitar."

"Why didn't you tell me you were a musician?"

"I am not really serious about it. I took piano lessons when I was young and learned to play the guitar, but not very well. Not like you and Frank. I couldn't keep up with you guys. It was good exercise for my fingers when I was learning to tie those surgical knots." He was glad to have an excuse to look at her without staring. She was so beautiful.

****

The time seemed to go by rather fast. The motor home was so luxurious and comfortable; it was like they were on a train, rolling across West Texas. They went through Alpine and on to Sanderson and headed toward the Rio Grande. "That must be Amistad Lake. That wasn't here when I was growing up here."

"It has about put our little ole Del Rio on the map. Thousands of tourists come here to fish and boat on that lake. It's right on the border. I guess the international border is in the center of the lake. Gives new meaning to the term 'wet back!'" Anna

Maria was giving the tour guide spiel. Everyone laughed at her irreverent comment. Especially since half of the group was Hispanic.

"Pull off when you see a place, Vicky. I might as well take it the rest of the way. I know right where to go." Cali was standing behind her partner waiting for her to stop the big bus. Vicky stopped and got up and exchanged places with her. Chui got up and followed Vicky to the back and Anna Maria sat in his place. Chui followed Vicky like a little puppy. They sat down together on the couch.

Chui looked out the big picture windows of the RV as they drove past familiar places. He had not been there for many years, but it all began to come back. Cali expertly maneuvered the bus around, down the familiar road toward the ranch. She turned into the long lane that seemed to have no end. Above them passed the big, well-worn, old wooden sign that announced the entrance to the "ITURRIA RANCH." Another sign had been added in the ensuing years. It said "ALOE VERA RANCH. HOME OF VASQUEZ ALOE VERA PRODUCTS."

No one spoke as the big vehicle squeezed its way down the lane. The big cottonwood trees were hanging over and making a scratching sound on the top and sides. The distance was about a half mile to the ranch house. It seemed like a long way to Chui. He was anxious. He didn't know what to expect. Everyone around him seemed to know more than he did. He had asked some questions, but he had so many more to ask. He had some questions that he hadn't even thought about yet. He looked over to Vicky and smiled. "You haven't ever been here?"

"No. This is my first trip, but it seems like I have. I sure have heard a lot about this ranch. Dr. Vasquez and I have had a lot of time together. She has told me all about it. Maybe you could show me around."

Chui was thinking the same thought. He desperately wanted to be alone with Vicky. He didn't even know why. He did not know what had happened to him in the last twenty-four hours, but he needed to find out what was going on.

It was just about high noon when the big bus finally rounded the last curve in the little narrow lane that led back to the ranch house. It suddenly opened up like a big valley as everyone looked out the windows. There on the porch was a black woman waving frantically. The RV stopped at the edge of the circle drive as the air brakes let out a final gush of air, as though to say "we finally made it." The side door opened and out rushed Anna Maria, grabbing her old partner and hugging her ever so tightly. "It is so good to see you, Dee Dee. Where's Momma?"

"Oh, she's coming. She will be here in a minute or two. You know it takes her a little while longer than it used to."

The remainder of the entourage stepped off the bus and walked toward the front porch. Aranda Vasquez came out the big front door with her arms out, ready to hug whoever was first and closest. It was Chui. He seemed so tall and she seemed so small and frail to him. He didn't want to squeeze her too tightly but he suddenly realized just how much he missed his grandmother. He remembered how she always put up with him and spoiled him and loved him unconditionally. She always found some good in him, when other's found it difficult. He walked up the few steps to the porch and put his hands on his grandmother's shoulders. "Abuela Randa. I missed you so much. I never forgot you. I am so happy to be here. Let me just hug you for a while." And with that he began to hug her and she placed her head on his chest and let the tears flow like they had been bottled up for years. She sobbed and so did Chui.

Frank and Cali stood together off to one side as they watched the reunion between Chui and his grandmother. Anna Maria and Dee Dee were energetically engaged in conversation. Vicky stood alone. She politely let this family do its greeting without her interference. She felt a little left out, but knew that was going to happen when they got here. She watched Chui as he finally let his grandmother loose from his grip. Randa dried her eyes with a lace handkerchief from the pocket of her sweater. Chui took his grandmother by the hand and led her over to Vicky. "Vicky, this is my Grandmother Randa. She is one of the most special people in my life." Vicky took Randa's hand and pressed it between her two hands as she kissed her on the cheek.

"I can see that, Mrs. Vasquez. I can see why you are so special to him."

"Well, first of all, let's stop with the 'Mrs. Vasquez' stuff. You will call me Abuela Randa or Grandma Randa, or whatever you want. Anything, but Mrs. Vasquez. That makes me sound old." They all laughed at the elderly lady's sharp wit. Vicky suddenly did not look at all like a seasoned Doctor of Medicine. She looked like a little girl who was just given a lollypop. She smiled that beautiful smile. Chui nearly melted -- again.

****

The ranch house looked like it was ready for a party – a big party. There were flowers everywhere. The table was decorated with a white linen tablecloth and all the fine silver and china. Someone with expertise in that area had, obviously, professionally decorated the place. "Dee Dee will take you to your rooms. We have the Mexican house all ready for some of you. We have plenty of rooms. This is a big house." Aranda was giving everyone directions as they brought their belongings into the big ranch house from the RV.

After everyone had gotten somewhat settled, Chui found Vicky outside, looking through the big window into the springhouse. "Boy, Grandma has certainly redone this house. Let's go in and look around." Chui had his chance to be alone with his heartthrob for a few minutes, at least.

"Would you like to show me around the place?"

"Sure. Absolutely. I would love to." Chui took her by the hand and headed toward the big barn-like shed where the horses were stabled. "You want to ride a horse?"

"Oh, Chui. I don't think I know how. I know you were raised on a horse on this ranch. But I grew up with cars and bicycles. How about one of these?" Vicky was pointing towards a green John Deere four-wheel drive vehicle parked outside the barn. 'This looks like more my style."

"Boy, this is something new. We sure didn't have these when I lived here. Looks like a Green Machine. I'll bet you don't have to feed them or give 'em a rest. But you can't tell 'em your troubles or sing to 'em either." He sang a bad version of "Back in the Saddle Again." Vicky laughed as she seated herself in the passenger side of the little green car. He turned the ignition and the vehicle started on the first try. "Well, my dear, let's check out the back forty." The couple sped away in their green machine – out past the big aloe factory and onto a trail that had only two tracks with grass growing in the center. They were finally getting away by themselves.

Chapter 60

"Laughlin tower, this is Heineken zero niner Yankee."

"Go ahead Heineken. What can we do for you today, sir?"

"You have a couple of old retired jet jocks up here in their private little airplane. We both learned to fly right here at Laughlin. Could we have a little latitude to fly around the edge of your zone? We just wanted to do a little sightseeing before we land at Del Rio International."

"Heineken, I have you on the screen. You don't look like you are in anyone's way up there. Where do you want to go?"

"We would just like to have a little latitude on our altitude over that big ranch north of the base. It belongs to my family. I wanted to say hello to them."

"Are you telling me you want to do a little buzz job, zero niner Yankee?"

"Couldn't put it better myself, Laughlin. Couldn't put it better."

"Nothing much I can do about it, is there? I don't see any traffic anywhere in the area. Not expecting any for quite a while. Have yourself a good day, sir. And – thanks for your service. We owe a lot to you old jet jockeys. Stay safe. Laughlin tower out."

Chapter 61

The back forty, as it was sometimes called, is rocky and hilly. But running through it is a beautiful stream that comes from the small mountains off in a distance, ending up in the Rio Grande River. It has strewn along it a ribbon of green trees and plants. Some huge Cottonwood trees adorn its banks. The stream is not wide, but it does run full most of the year. The green machine approached the green foliage. The old family cemetery is fenced off, atop a hill, near the stream. "This is where I loved to come when I was a kid. I would ride my horse out here sometimes and just enjoy the day and read the gravestones. These are my ancestors. They died to get in here. Some of them have been here a while."

Vicky chuckled at his humor. "It is so beautiful out here, Chui. Let's get out and walk around a little."

The two figures were suddenly holding hands as they walked. It felt good to both of them. It was the first evidence of their burgeoning relationship. "Let's go see your family cemetery, Chui. I would love to see it."

They walked through the gate of the fenced off area. Chui found his grandfather, Paco's, grave immediately. It was the most recent. He paused a few seconds and let a few memories of his demanding old Abuelo pass through his mind. They wandered through the head stones. Some of them were from the 1700's and were nearly illegible. "You know, Chui, for centuries, Chinese people would never marry outside of their culture or nationality. I don't see any names, other than Hispanics on these graves. I suppose their traditions were the same."

"Well, they were until I came along." Chui laughed. "They called me a Coyote, when I was born. That is just another name for 'half-breed'!"

"Well, I sure think that is a ridiculous tradition in this day and age. The Anglos eventually married the Saxons, you know. And I'll bet your mother has all sorts of different nationalities in her blood."

"Would your family expect you to marry a Chinese man?" Chui asked a loaded question.

Vicky gave him her biggest sexiest smile ever as she turned toward him and said, "I certainly hope not, Chui. It wouldn't do them any good. I will marry whomever I want."

There was a long silence as the two figures left the cemetery and headed down the hill toward the little babbling stream and the big cottonwood trees. Vicky spoke first. "I like you, Chui." It was unexpected but gave him a nice warm ripple down his back. He had been holding her hand, but gently slipped his hand around her waist and eased her a little closer as they walked along the stream toward the big cottonwood tree. She didn't resist. She put her arm around his waist.

"Vicky, I don't know what to say. I have been trying to figure out what I am feeling since I first laid eyes on you yesterday." He drew her a bit closer as they walked together in lockstep. "You are a doctor with a good career. You are my mother's partner. I am a homeless alcoholic. You saw what happened to me last night. I got the DT's. Let's call it what it is. I thought I had bugs crawling on me. I thought I was having a heart attack."

"Chui." Her voice became a whisper. "I am a doctor, for sure. I do have a career, but I treat alcoholics. I understand. I knew exactly what you were experiencing. Your job is to get well and you have a lot of good help, including me. But be that as it may, I like you and would like to stay in touch with you." They reached the big cottonwood tree and Vicky turned around and leaned against the tree and looked up at him.

"Vicky, I like you too. I am really attracted to you. But it has been a long time since I deserved a woman's attention. I just haven't been very desirable. I am just a drunk, Vicky, just a good-for-nothing drunk"

"Chui, will you shush." She reached up and was about to give him a gentle kiss on the cheek. He grabbed her around the waist and pulled her close to him. He slid his arms up behind her head and kissed her softly – then harder and harder -- as he pushed her gently back to the cottonwood tree. Their temperance was about to be thrown to the wind – he was about to slide his hands down her back and touch her where he shouldn't but where she desperately wanted him to. And just as his hands reached the back of that short, blue skirt that was really shorts, and were about to roam around where he had been wanting to roam around for the past two days ------ ZOOOOM! ---- The loudest noise they had heard in their lives interrupted them just at the crucial moment. They separated, jumped back and looked up to the sky. It was a huge Heineken beer can that looked like a jet plane. The jet swished by like a crop duster about fifty feet from the ground and pulled up and returned for another pass. This time is slowed down a bit and came close enough to see the two pilots and three passengers inside waving at them.

The couple held each other by the waist as they ambled back toward the green machine. "That was close." Chui squeezed Vicky's belt line.

"You mean the jet plane or the sex? I didn't think it was quite close enough." She grinned at her double meaning. "You likee me and I likee you too big music man. We come back and see tlees and backee forty sometime and come no flyplane next time. OK?"

Chui couldn't believe his ears -- even though it was Pigin. He loved her jokes. He had waited a lifetime for this situation. He just knew he had died and this was heaven. He didn't care. He had never been happier than this moment. Vicky seemed to share the same feeling. They drove the green machine back to the ranch house, each with a smile that was not removable. They were in love – hopelessly in love. And it was a perfect day. She was unconsciously humming a song as they rode the few miles back to the ranch house. He heard and recognized the song, but didn't comment. He let her hum. She was humming "Body and Soul."

Chapter 62

"Did you see that idiot that was buzzing the ranch? I thought he was going to crash in the back forty. He scared us to death." Chui was relating the story to his family, not having any idea who it was or why they did it.

"Did you get a tour of the ranch?" Chui's mother was asking Vicky. She somehow suspected there was more than just an inspection of the property involved. She could see the radiance in her partner's face. She could feel the radiance in her son's soul. She was a happy friend and mother. She knew it was strange, but it was fine. It was better than fine. It was wonderful.

"Chui and I checked out the green machine. He showed me the back forty. It is beautiful out there. We came back when we thought we were being invaded by the Heineken Air Force." Everyone thought her joke was hilarious. Everyone knew why the plane was buzzing the ranch – except Chui. But he was about to find out.

About an hour later a van pulled into the circle drive. It had been rented from the Del Rio Airport. All the members of the family had been cautiously gazing out the big picture window now and then. "Wonder who that might be?" Anna Maria announced slyly. "We better go out and check it out. C'mon, Chui."

316

They all walked out to greet the van and its passengers. First out was the smallest of the group. He still had on his flight suit with the Heineken logo prominently displayed on his chest. Chui looked him over. Something was trying to connect – but had not yet. *"Heineken beer – Heineken beer can – jet plane – buzzing the ranch."* Chui was trying to put it all together, but he didn't know quite what was going on. He remembered his mother talking about his dad -- working for a brewery in Amsterdam. He didn't remember who it was. He didn't drink beer – he drank vodka.

Cali finally got between Chui and the smaller man with the flight suit. "Chui. We have been saving this little surprise for you. I would like for you to meet Johnny Vanstreen. He had to change his identity. He was born right here in this ranch house. His name back then was Juan Jesus Vasquez. Chui, this is your dad."

Chui was about out of emotions for the day. The two men moved toward each other slowly. Then they picked up speed and came together like a couple of linemen at a Super Bowl game. "Chui, Chui, Chui," Johnny could not say his son's name enough times. "I have so much to tell you. I have so much to apologize for. I have waited for this moment for years." The two grown men looked at each other and tried not to believe what the years had done to each of them. There was Johnny's son, now an older man where a teenage kid stood the last time he saw him. There was a grayed haired, wrinkled man in his seventies, where

317

Chui's dad had once stood and bragged about his accomplishments, and joked with his Grandpa Williams.

"God damn you people. I am going to be cried out for the next year if you don't stop doing this to me." Chui looked at his father's flight suit and the Heineken's beer can on his pocket. "Did you just about knock me out of the back forty about an hour ago? Yes, you did, you sonofagun – it's starting to make sense now."

"Sorry about that. I just wanted to have a closer look and scare a few sheep. Like the old days." He flashed his big Mexican smile.

Chapter 63

The other passengers were emerging from the van. The two older men got out with some difficulty. Cali took Chui by the hand and led him to them. "And here is Uncle Ramon and Damon." They hugged and kissed each other. "We are not finished yet. You can hug them some more in a few minutes."

Johnny took over. "I want you to meet my significant other, Robin Vanstreen. We have been partners for many years, Chui. We are a gay couple. We have lived in Holland for years. I took his name when your aunt killed me off and got me out of the CIA and gave me a new life. I hope you are OK with that."

"Of course, Dad. It's the 21st century. I think it's great." Things were moving so fast, Chui was having trouble keeping up with everything. It was almost anticlimactic. His head was spinning as he tried to take everything in.

By this time, Dee Dee had joined the festivities. "And who else is in the van?" The other man had been sitting in the back seat. No one had noticed him yet. "Anna Maria. Come over here!" She pulled her long time friend toward the door of the van as the man was backing out. No one could see his face yet. Just as Anna

Maria and Dee Dee arrived at the door of the van, the man turned around to face them.

Anna Maria screamed at the top of her lungs. "Oh, my God. Oh, my God. I can't believe this. You little shit!" she turned to her friend. Then back to the man. "Dallas – Dallas – Dallas. Dallas King."

She hugged and hugged, tighter and tighter. He returned the hug. "I have missed you so much." She buried her face in his chest and he kissed her on top of the head.

"You ain't missed me any more than I missed you, Darlin'. I'm just glad to be on the damn ground. That brother of yours about scared the crap out of me. He thought he was flyin' an old cotton crop duster." She loved his Texas dialect. They walked arm in arm toward the porch. Aranda Vasquez was standing on the porch, like a Maestro, taking it all in. She was watching the festivities, smiling and letting the tears run down her cheeks. She had orchestrated this event and now everyone was enjoying the concert. She had been looking forward to this day for many weeks.

Chapter 64

Just as the group was about to go into the big ranch house, another vehicle pulled into the circle drive. It was a white Lincoln, about three years old. Dee Dee Washington ran out ahead of the crowd to open the door of the car. A rather large, very dark black man got out. He was dressed in a well-tailored suit with a stiff-starched white shirt and maroon tie. His shoes were shined to a mirror finish. He had a handkerchief in his pocket. He retrieved a bouquet of roses from the seat. Dee Dee seemed to know who he was. She came around to the open door and he greeted her. "I brought you some flowers."

"Oh. Thank you. They are so pretty. Did you have any trouble finding the place?"

"No. Your directions were just perfect."

The group was suddenly silent – waiting for some sort of information about this stranger. "I have a little surprise for you all. I would like you to meet a new friend of mine. This is Charles Marley. He is the minister at the Baptist Church in Del Rio. He comes from Jamaica." Everyone waited for someone else to break the silence.

"Well, it's about time." It was Randa who spoke first. "I thought my day was perfect, but this

321

puts the cork in the bottle. This just puts the icing on the cake. This puts the ---"

"We understand, Momma. " Anna Maria was laughing at her mother's quips. "Would you like to tell us what has been going on, my dear partner? Why didn't you tell me about Charles, here? I thought we had no secrets." The black man looked a little uncomfortable. Dee Dee put him at ease as she explained that they had met in the library. He was reading history books about other religions and so was Dee Dee. They both grabbed the same book. That prompted a discussion about religion. When he revealed that he was a Baptist preacher, she couldn't believe it. "Then I told him I was an ex nun and he about fell on the floor. We almost got kicked out of the library from laughing. Everyone kept telling us to shush. We weren't supposed to be reading such stuff, neither of us." Dee Dee was laughing as she told the story. "He grew up in Kingston and went to a missionary school sponsored by the Baptist Church." She looked at him and he flashed his white teeth and shook his head in agreement.

"Well, first of all, I am so hoppy to met you." His Jamaican dialect was evident. "I get to the States and get a job singing with a Rastafarian Reggae band while I was going to a Baptist college." He explained that his life was a little incongruous.

"So you are a musician, too?" It was Frank who took a sudden interest in his background.

322

"Yeah, Mon. I learn to play the steel drum and then the guitar. But I also sing. But that was awhile ago. Now I am the minister at the little Calvary Baptist church in Del Rio. I even get Delores to come on Sunday mornings. She sings in my choir. She is a good gospel singer."

Dee Dee hung her head as though someone had just given away one of her well kept secrets.

"Well you little shit." It was Anna Marie who irreverently chastised her old friend. "I am so happy for you. No wonder you called Dallas. You didn't want me to be alone, did you?"

Dee Dee's black face sparkled with impishness. "Well, *I* knew you wanted me to call him. *You* just didn't know."

Old Aranda Vasquez knew all about it. She knew about everything. She was the mastermind of this reunion. She had worked on this event for weeks. But she had one final chore. She called everyone into the huge living room. "I want you all to know how happy I am that you could all come and appease this old woman. I do not know how much longer I have on this planet. I needed to tidy up a few things. That is why we are all here. Frank. Father Francisco. Father Ortiz y Jimenez." She called Frank by all the names he had used over the past years of his life. "I know you need to say something."

Chapter 65

Frank stood up and, nervously, looked around. He cleared his throat, but his voice was still tight. "I have preached many thousands of masses and sermons and weddings and christenings and so many other things I can't remember them all. But this might be the most difficult speech I have ever given." He paused and took a breath. No one made a sound.

"I need to talk about something that might be a little delicate." He directed his attention to Chui. "It might be something you would just as soon not hear, Chui. None of us wants to hear intimate things about our parents. It is natural. But you need to know the real story." He stood up and faced Chui directly as he spoke. "Exactly fifty-five years ago today -- It was March 24th, 1950. I will never forget that day. It changed my life. Now I need to get it changed back to where it should have been." Frank paused again and Chui grew a little uncomfortable. He was sitting next to Vicky. She grabbed his hand and held it tightly.

"I need to tell you about a trip to South Padre Island way back in 1950. I had organized a kind of 'Spring Break.'" He looked at Johnny and then at Cali, then back to Chui. "Your mother and I had been flirting with each other for some time. I thought it was fun and certainly gave me an ego trip. But -- I was getting a little concerned with her teen-age crush. I thought I needed to do something to stop it. So -- I asked her mother, your grandmother, to go along on the trip. I did that on purpose. Cali nodded in response. "Everything went just fine until my drinking began to interfere with my judgment. Cali's mother, Grandma Susie, and I came very close to getting into a terrible situation on the beach. Fortunately I had the good sense to stop it before it got started. We were supposed to be the chaperones, but we were letting our students smoke grass while we were drinking wine and playing kissey face games up the beach. Chui was squirming around in his chair. He looked down toward the floor. He was not comfortable.

"Chui, I know this is not pleasant. But you have to know what happened. I know this is embarrassing but just let me finish." He stopped to regain his thoughts. "After Cali's mother, Susie -- your grandmother – passed out from too much wine, I helped her back to the little cabana and put her on the top bunk. I went back to the students on the beach around the fire. I found Cali and Johnny under a blanket wrapped up together. At that time I had no idea about Johnny's sexual preference." Now Johnny was looking down at the floor. Robin patted him on the shoulder and he smiled.

"When I pulled them apart, Cali was bare-chested and was pretty high on grass." Cali stared toward the ceiling without looking at anything. Now she was getting very uncomfortable with the story. "So, when I told her to get up and get away from Johnny, she grabbed my arm and dragged me down the beach for a few hundred feet into the darkness. We staggered around and ran behind some big sand dunes and fell on the sand and she began to peel off my shirt." Frank began to lose his composure. He paused and took a deep breath. He struggled to get the words out. "I finally have the guts to tell the truth about that night. I have been denying it for fifty-five years." He fought off the emotion long enough to choke out the words. "We made love on the beach that night. I violated a high school girl that I was supposed to be protecting." He tried in vane to rationalize. "I had a lot of wine that night. But, that was no excuse. I knew it was wrong. I knew it was against my religion, my vows and my morals. But I couldn't help it. I couldn't stop. I loved her so much. I really did. I had been in love with her since I first met her. But she was Johnny's girl and I was a priest. But I couldn't help myself. I was very young then." Frank's voice was nearly drowned out by his sobs as he went over to Cali, knelt down on the floor and put his head on her shoulder and sobbed. She ran her fingers through his white hair.

The group was politely silent, waiting for the next shoe to drop. He finally stood up straight. He went over to Chui. "Chui -- stand up! I need to tell you something I should have said fifty-five years ago this Christmas." Chui stood up and faced the priest. "Chui. Johnny Vasquez or Vanstreen, your dad, is probably the most

326

wonderful man I have ever known. He is a saint. He tried to save my life. He tried to save my career. He only succeeded in getting himself into trouble and paid for it. I cannot say enough good things about your father."

Frank groped for the words. He took a very long breath. Chui was seeing him in a totally different light. He was not the resolute priest who chastised him after he fell off the wagon and got drunk two days ago. He was not the big strong man with the white beard who could play piano better than anyone he had ever known. His voice was trembling. Right now he looked weak and helpless. Chui suddenly felt very sorry for him.

Frank gestured toward Johnny. "This man did his very best to raise you as well as he could. He suffered an enormous sacrifice. I threw him an unbelievable burden and he took it. I owe him my life. And he was the best father to you he knew how to be." Frank paused as though he needed one more breath to say what he had to say. It came out of his mouth like a pent-up sneeze. "But he is *not* your father, Chui!" Then the words choked out. The two words he had been needing to say for years. "I AM! I am your father, Chui. I am your father and I am so sorry it took me all these years to take responsibility for it. I am so sorry I let someone else take my responsibilities. I am so glad I finally was able to find you and tell you. You are so much a part of me. I am so proud of you." It was as though Frank couldn't get his words to stop. He had been holding back this confession for fifty-five years and now it was erupting. He kept repeating the words over and over, through the sobbing, as his voice finally faded away into silence. He sat down beside Cali and continued sobbing. She put her arm around him.

The group finally began to whisper a little among themselves. Chui stood with a blank stare looking at Frank. Vicky snatched his arm and steadied him.

Frank calmed himself and continued. "You see, your grandfather and I gave you a double dose of musical talent. But I gave you that terrible alcoholic disease. I was the most selfish human on the face of the earth. I let your dad take the blame for my deed. I let him pay my way. I let him support you. I owe him a huge debt, which I can never repay. I rationalized. I drank my brains out, played games with myself and ran away. I tried to forget you. I pretended it was not true. I tried to put it out of my mind. But I couldn't. I desperately needed to find you, Chui – my only begotten son – and make amends before I cash in and go to my rewards."

Chui was numb. He didn't know what to say or do. He looked around at the group and everyone was watching him – they were waiting for some sort of reaction. All he wanted to do right now was to go away and be alone for a while. Very briefly he thought he needed a drink. But he quickly dismissed that thought. He needed to digest this sudden, abrupt turn of events in his new life. He let go of Vicky's hand and got up and ran out onto the big ranch house porch. Johnny followed him outside. They leaned against the wooden porch railing. "That was quite a dose of news, wasn't it? I know you are having trouble getting it all straight in your mind His dad – his former dad – put his arm around Chui's shoulder. "I have known about this since you were born." He made an effort to soothe Chui's emotions.

"But why. Dad? Why didn't you tell me? Why let me think --?"

"Chui. We were all selfish and looking out for our own interests – All of us. Your mom wanted to get back at her parents for what she thought they did to her. I wanted to prove to the world that I was normal and could get the prettiest girl in school – when I was really kidding myself. I was born gay and nothing could change that. And Frank. He was a catholic priest. He gave a vow of celibacy and morality and all the other things that priests do. He certainly couldn't step forward and tell the truth. I was a devout catholic boy. And so it seemed the right thing to do. We would all just let it go and it would work out. But we forgot one thing." He paused for a second and faced Chui. "We forgot about you, Chui. And a few days ago, after we finally found you, we all agreed we needed to do something to correct that. We needed to pay you back for all the lies we lived at your expense."

Chui was looking out into the big front yard, remembering his childhood, playing in that lawn and thinking about what he had just heard. "Chui! Just look at me. I am proud of my heritage. But my ancestors are Yaqui Indians. I am small and wiry. I don't even shave. I have no facial hair. I'm a great pilot, but I have no musical talent. Look at Frank. He is tall and true, upper class Spanish from Spain. He is a gifted musician. Chui, you look just like him. You talk like him. You even act like him. He has always wanted to be your father. And now he truly is."

"What about Grandma Randa? When did she know about this?"

"Probably longer than anyone knew." Johnny chuckled a little at his comment about his mother. "But your grandfather, Paco, never knew. He didn't know about your mom or me, either. He would have had a real problem with all this. It's just as well he never knew. And your real grandparents -- Grandpa Jim figured it out long ago but your Grandmother Susie never knew the truth. We left it that way. Your Grandpa Jim Williams was a saint, Chui. He was a real saint. He was better and kinder to me than my own father would ever have been. I can't say enough good things about him." Chui gave Johnny a long tender hug. They pulled apart.

"Thanks, Dad. I think I am about ready to go in now." The two men walked back inside the big

living room and faced the group. Chui walked
over to Frank.

"I'm sorry I ran out, I needed a little time to
think." Chui looked up at the ceiling, as if to get
some inspiration from somewhere. He looked back
at Frank. "I just need to tell you a few things, now.
First of all I want you to know this." Frank had
no idea what he was going to hear but he was
ready for whatever it was. Frank stood up. Chui
paused for a short time and cleared his throat. He
smiled at Frank and touched his arm. "It's OK,
Frank. That's what I want you to know - it's OK."
Chui faced Frank and looked into his face.
"Frank. – Uh – Father Frank -- Dad?" He looked
over to Johnny, who gave him the OK sign with his
thumb and finger. "I need to tell you that my life
has not been perfect. You know all about that
now. It has been pretty damn lousy sometimes.
But it is no more your fault than it is – uh --
Charlie's – and I just met him today." The black
man laughed and showed his white teeth. "All I
can say to you is...I am a big boy. I was
responsible for my own actions, not you." He
turned and faced the group. He paused, again as if
to gather his thoughts. "Today, I want you all to
know four days ago I was ready to take my own
life. I didn't care to live any longer. But right
now, I am the happiest man in the world. I have
my family. I have my Vicky. I have new friends.
A long list of people has thought enough of me to
go to enormous lengths to rescue me and bring me
back to life." He turned back toward Frank.
"And you, Frank – you alone – are at the top of

that list." Chui smiled and held his arms out like a preacher -- one toward Johnny's and one toward Frank. "Hell, I think it is wonderful to have two fathers. It makes me feel special. Most people only have one." Someone chuckled. "Frank – you gave me back my life. I love you. But, first and foremost – I *forgive* you. *What is -- is. What is* can't be changed. We can't take it back." He put his arms around the priest and hugged him for a long time.

Frank regained his composure and took a breath. "Chui. I couldn't ask for a better son than you." He cleared his throat. "Now that we have formed this mutual admiration society -- I just need to ask one favor."

Chui couldn't imagine what his new father wanted to ask him. "Sure. What is that, Frank – uh Dad – who-the-hell-ever you are?" The group laughed and broke the serious tension of the last few minutes.

"I need to ask your permission to marry your mother."

There was a long pause. "Holy shit! You friggin' priest!" Chui's irreverent retort slipped out of his mouth. "For God's sake – you are my *dad.* You can marry my *mom* if you want. Hell yes. Great idea -- go for it! You are sleeping with her anyway, aren't you?" The whole family began to laugh loudly.

After this remark, Chui had one more question. He thought he needed to address the whole group, to be certain he got the right person. "May I ask one more thing?" The group got quiet. "I have an envelope in my saxophone case that has changed my life. It gave me confidence to do what I couldn't do before. It gave me faith in people. It made me proud of myself. It made me responsible for myself. I am not a religious man, but it restored my faith in people." He excused himself and quickly went to his room and retrieved the envelope with the money. He brought it back into the living room unopened. He laid it on the table and shouted out loud. "WHO THE HELL GAVE ME THIS MONEY? WHERE DID IT COME FROM? WHO PUT IT THERE? WHY? WILL SOMEONE EXPLAIN IT TO ME?"

There was a long silence. Finally his grandmother rose up from her chair, where she had been sitting through all the serious dialogue of the past several minutes. Dee Dee started to help her and she waved her off. She hobbled, unaided, over to the big table where Chui had laid the envelope. She carefully opened the big envelope and began to count the hundred dollar bills. It took several minutes, but everyone was patient and quiet as she silently counted to herself, moving her lips but not speaking out loud. She looked up at everyone watching her. "Fifty thousand dollars! Exactly. Fifty thousand dollars. You did not spend a penny. Not a penny, Chui."

"I didn't need to. Money kept coming at me from everywhere -- not only money, but also fame and fortune and love and new friendships and family. Everything good kept happening to me. I didn't seem to have any control over it. Somehow, I just didn't need any of that money. It changed my life and I didn't even spend it!"

"I knew you wouldn't need it, Chui. That is why I gave it to you. I had it drawn from a bank in El Paso and gave it to Frank to give to his Hindu friend, the hotel man, to put in your little doorway. You could have spent it – and that would have been fine. It was yours. You could have drunk it away – that was your choice." His grandmother paused for a few seconds. "But you didn't. You thought someone lost it. I'll bet you even tried to find its owner. That was your first concern. You used it to get back your life. And you didn't even need to spend it – not a penny. That tells me something about you, Chui." Everyone was silent as Aranda Vasquez spoke to her grandson. "I guess you have figured out by now, you have never been truly blood related to me. But that doesn't matter to me. I have known you were not my own flesh and blood for many years now. But I don't care about that. It's not important to me. You were a loving and kind Nieto. I still love you just for who you are." She put the money back in the envelope and handed it back to Chui. "It's yours to start your new life." Then, like detective Colombo, she turned around. "Oh – one more thing..."

334

Then she turned and hobbled over to the big sideboard cupboard and opened a drawer. She removed an old leather pouch, which was tied with leather thongs. "Chui. I want you to look at these documents." She pulled out an old worn parchment that was quite old. "This is the deed to this ranch. And these are my stocks – giving me controlling interest in the Vasquez Aloe Corporation." She took one last look at the papers and then handed them to Chui. "Every member of this family has been tremendously successful in their lives. Their share of the Aloe Company has paid them and me quite handsomely. They are all well into their seventies and do not need to worry about their futures. None of them has any children. No one to leave it to. And so – with everyone's consent and agreement -- I have signed these all over to you. It is yours now, Chui. Everything. You are now the sole owner of the Iturria Ranch and have controlling interest in the Aloe Vera Company which your old grandfather, Paco, founded all those years ago."

Chui couldn't speak. He just stared at the pouch and the papers for a few seconds, trying to understand what had just happened to him. He looked around the room. Everyone was smiling and nodding in agreement. Then his grandmother quipped, "You can change the name of this ranch if you want. That old sign out there has been there forever. I wanted to change it for years, but stubborn old Paco wouldn't let me!" She chuckled at her humor.

"But Abuela, I am not even related to you. You heard Frank."

"Shush." She put her finger over his mouth and smiled at him. "We already went through that, didn't we? Better put the papers back in that that pouch and put it somewhere safe. Put it in your saxophone case. That seems to be a good place. My lawyers have already taken care of the details, but you might want to keep the deed. It's an antique!"

Aranda Vasquez paused and surveyed the situation. She wiped her hands unconsciously on her little apron. Her old, wrinkled, brown face was tired, but happy. She had orchestrated this reunion down to the last detail. She looked around as if she was making sure nothing was left undone. She was satisfied that everything had been accomplished just as it was planned. She blew out a big breath. "Now then." She addressed the family and guests. "I have been wanting to have a party around here for the last fifty-five years. Let's have one now. Wouldn't old Paco roll over in his grave if he knew what was going on in his ranch house today? Just look here. We got a black Baptist preacher and a turncoat, Anglican priest. We got two ex-nuns and two doctors. Now, wouldn't he be surprised at little runaway Cali. He thought you were a hippy doing drugs somewhere." She gave Caliente a little kiss on the cheek as she spoke. "We got two gay pilots, two old retired marines and an old Texas Ranger and CIA agent. And I just gave his ranch away to a man he disowned, who wasn't even related to him." She turned to Delores. "Dee Dee. Make me some tea. Let's get on with the party!"

Chapter 66 -- The present

Anna Maria Vasquez and Dallas King are living in Clearwater Beach at his home. She was a virgin when they met but now they love to go out in the fishing boat and sometimes make love on the boat when they think no one is watching.

Delores Washington married her Baptist preacher, Charlie Marley. Father Frank performed the ceremony. Charlie still sings Reggae music and plays the steel drums. Delores teaches a class in comparative religion at the community college. Her students are very much aware of her previous life as a nun. She still sings in the Baptist Church gospel choir. She also attends mass.

Ramon and Damon Vasquez returned to their home at the VA Hospital Center in Clearwater Beach, Florida. They are active in their little military community. They meet with other veterans every day and exchange old war stories. They tell the same stories over and over, but no one remembers, so that's OK.

Johnny and Robin Vanstreen are still living in Key West, Florida. They are openly gay and it is OK. They were married in Mallory Square at sunset by Father Frank in a ceremony attended by the whole family. Johnny and Robin flew everyone there in the Heineken Beer-Can jet for the wedding. They regularly go to Sloppy Joe's, drink Heineken beer and eat boiled shrimp.

Dr. Caliente Susanne Williams Vasquez married her lifelong friend and recent lover-- Father Francisco Ortiz y Jimenez. Charlie Marley, the Baptist minister, from Jamaica, performed the ceremony. They were married at the old ranch house. She retired from the medical profession and turned her motor home over to her partner, Dr. Vicky Chen. Dr. Vasquez and Father Frank live in Santa Fe, New Mexico. But they have a summer home at South Padre Island, Texas. He has been known to play at some of the local Padre Island watering holes, entertaining the older folks by imitating Nat King Cole. He wears his red shirt during these occasions. It has become his trademark. He still attends AA meetings every day. His wife, Caliente, walks on the beach every day. The Jetties Restaurant has long since been torn down, but its memories are still there for them both.

Chui Vasquez and Dr. Vicky Chen returned to that cottonwood tree in the back forty the very next day before they left the ranch. This time there were no interruptions. They drove the green machine and stocked it with plenty of blankets and food for the journey. She had a small glass of wine and he drank soda water with lime. They stayed all day. They now live in Albuquerque, where she continues to practice medicine. They have a cabin in the Sangre de Cristo Mountains outside Santa Fe. Father Frank married them at the old ranch in the back forty by the cottonwood tree. The whole family came to the wedding, including his other father, Johnny Vanstreen. Cali and Vicky are now more than just partners. Vicky is now her daughter-in-law and Cali her mother-in-law. Since her name is now "Vasquez," Vicky was able to keep Dr. V's Mobile Medical Center intact, without changing the lettering on the side. She has used her new husband and his new father as voluntary subjects in the study of alcoholism. She has presented professional papers and has been in demand as a speaker at medical conventions. Since she is a physician, she has access to fertility drugs. She has been secretly taking them and crossing her fingers. She hopes to have some good news for her husband very soon. They believe that a child, which is a mixture of Spanish, European and Chinese, would be a wonderful combination. She still sometimes speaks Pigin English just to make everyone laugh.

Chui has not had a drink since the Capri Lounge in 2005. He plays in Santa Fe with his father as frequently as possible. Their drink of choice is soda water with lime.

Chui has become a skilled businessman and has invested his money very wisely. He is on the board of directors of several successful corporations. Many of these corporations are recording companies. He has played studio music for numerous recording stars. He and Vicky often visit his mother and father at Padre Island. He always looks forward to playing jazz with his father. He now understands why they played so well together from the very first note. He does not know why, but he knows they are able to read each other's minds while they are playing together. Occasionally he will play, *"Body and Soul,"* but only when his wife, Vicky, is there. He still has his old Selmer saxophone and his grandfather's old blue overcoat with the imprint of master sergeant stripes on the sleeves. He still keeps Punj's shirt, razor and toothbrush as a reminder of times past. He still has the robe, allegedly stolen from the Hilton Hotel in Chicago. He sends Punjabi Gupta fresh flowers and a gift certificate to Denny's every month -- just to wish him well and thank him for his important place in his life.

Aranda Cantu Vasquez died while napping early one Sunday morning at the age of 98. She was sitting in her favorite chair in the springhouse of the ranch. She was drinking some tea with just a tiny little brandy. She had a smile on her face. The squirrels were playing outside in the trees. Her entire family and all her friends and neighbors came for her funeral. They cried and mourned and then gave her a wake at the old ranch house. It was a wonderful party. She would have wanted it that way. Chui has a contract with a local flower shop to put fresh flowers on her grave every Sunday. The G & G law firm handles the arrangements for him.

Epilogue

Recently, Chui sold some of the ranch property to a developer. It netted him more money than anyone will divulge. The ranch house, the springhouse and the Mexican house and 50 acres of property were retained for the family. The remainder of the property has been turned into a successful gated, high end, residential development. As a memorial to his stubborn old grandfather, Paco, Chui decided *not* to change the original name. The developers named the new development "Iturria Ranch." The name was suggested by Chui. The residents have no idea where the name originated. Its entrance is now an automatic, electronic gate. But, the original carved wooden "Iturria Ranch" sign still hangs over it. It is the same entrance that has been there for nearly four hundred years.

The aloe business was merged with a major drug company for an undisclosed sum, but rumored to be several million dollars.

Aranda Vasquez is buried in the private family cemetery, which is surrounded by a high secure fence. It remains a family cemetery with its private entrance. Her grave is located next to

Paco, near an old cottonwood tree on the little stream in what was called the back forty.

Chui Vasquez purchased a small, but very secure, safe for his home. In it, he placed the leather pouch, which contains the original deed to the ranch. He also put an envelope in the safe. It contains $50,000 in hundred dollar bills. He has never spent a penny of it.

THE END